FINANCIAL FREEDOM

BEGINS IN YOUR HEART

NOT YOUR BANK ACCOUNT

FINANCIAL FREEDOM

BEGINS IN YOUR HEART
NOT YOUR BANK ACCOUNT

Diane M. Grubis

ISBN: 979-8-9910845-0-5

Interior Design by Gloria Erickson, London Lane Designs, Cover Design by Julia Arambam

Published in the United States of America.

Contents

Introduction

What is Financial Freedom?

"How could you lose $10,000?! Where did it all go?!" Bill and Holly walked into my financial planning office one winter day, looking tense at the thought of revealing their financial situation to a stranger. Bill made the appointment with me to start financial planning for his growing family. As I investigated their finances, I noticed that his wife, Holly, started to get nervous and looked away from me. In the process of discovery, I found a few things that didn't square up on their spreadsheet. We reviewed the numbers repeatedly, trying to understand the gap I was seeing. I asked them if there was any other income that may have been missing from their information. There was obviously $10,000 being spent over and above their household income per year. Slowly, the light bulb came into Bill's eyes, and Holly began to cry. Amidst incredulity, accusations, and tears, the couple departed from my office to talk privately.

Bill and Holly faced a problem that many people, whether married or single, deal with all too often. I believe the solution to this and many other financial issues is Financial Freedom through the Word of God.

What is financial freedom, and why should anyone pursue it? As a financial planner, the first question I'd ask my clients was what their goals and long-term desires were. Many people would answer that they wanted to be financially independent. They wanted to have enough money available in their bank accounts, in their investment properties, or in other accounts so they did not have to depend upon their job, other people, or even the government as their source. To most people, that sounds like a great goal. However, few people ever really achieve it. Why not? It's simple... Because life happens, people aren't perfect, and God was left out of their plans.

Money with a Purpose

Stop and ask yourself, "What is the purpose of my life and finances?" Perhaps you would say that my family is the most important thing in life, or my health is more vital than money. However, let's explore another vantage point for how to view wealth and even our life's value and purpose on this earth.

What moves you to tears? What angers you and begs for justice? Is it to abolish human trafficking, to provide clean water to third-world countries, or to create inventions to help people minister to patients in the medical field?

Financial freedom begins in your heart.

These problems, as noble as they are, require big solutions. Maybe it is to start your own business, or to send your kids to an exceptionally good school, or maybe to fix the washing machine that nags the living daylights out of you each time you use it! Big or small, worldwide or in your own home, what is the one thing that appears to be lacking that could solve all these problems? You are probably thinking MONEY, right? This is the answer most people would give. But, if I may tell you the truth, there are really two things missing - money and a wise, spiritually strong, forward-thinking YOU!

Financial Freedom Begins in Your Heart

The financial freedom I am talking about does not begin where you think it does—in your bank account, your job, or your higher education—it begins in your heart. It is in our hearts where God dwells and where the kingdom of God has come to live powerfully.

Join me, Bill, Holly, and many others on this life journey of faith toward financial freedom and discover the truth that will be revealed to us. "And you shall know the truth, and the truth shall make you free." (John 8:32). The truth we know, apply, and put into practice will make us free. And what does all this have to do with finances? Plenty! If our hearts are free, then:

- We are no longer in bondage.
- We are free to give.
- We are free to receive.
- We are free to manage all the goodness we are receiving.
- Finally, we are free to love God, partner with Him, and help others by going beyond ourselves and expanding God's Kingdom on this earth.

Walk with me past dusty roads of selfish desires and through treacherous forests of fear and dark valleys of ignorance, and let's come out together into heaven's wide-open spaces of bountiful living. Let's work toward the goal of building something great that will last for all of eternity!

Let's go!

Chapter 1

Financial Freedom Begins

"I can hear a heartbeat!" Lisa shouted as she listened excitedly through the doctor's stethoscope in his medical office. She was 20 weeks pregnant with her first baby! What a blessing and honor it is to be a mother. Although the father of her baby had abandoned them, Lisa knew with God's grace, she would be fine.

Lisa decided to live in her parents' basement, which was remodeled just for her, into a cute little apartment. How gracious of her parents to take her back into their home after she moved out on her own, drifted away from the Lord, and got involved with the wrong crowd. She truly came to the end of herself when she found out she was pregnant and carrying a precious baby in her womb. Through a lot of painful tears, turning back to God's grace, and sincere repentance, she mustered up all the courage she had and returned home to her loving parents. She was broken financially and drained physically and mentally. Lisa's parents prayed for her from the time she was born, and they knew she had a call of God on her life. They believed Lisa was destined for greater things than the life she was currently living.

Lisa accepted Jesus as her Lord and Savior while in junior high school. Shortly after that, she got involved with the wrong crowd, progressively made bad choices, and started to live a destructive lifestyle. The Word of God had been deposited in her heart through her parents, the teachings of her church's youth group, and through her own Bible reading. But it was not enough to combat the hurts and cares of this world that took root in her heart. The enemy came to steal the Word of God out of Lisa's heart and tried to kill and destroy God's plan for her life. He didn't win! The prayers of the saints prevailed, and Lisa returned to the arms of her loving Savior.

What was in Lisa's heart that caused her to turn away from God? Like many people today, Lisa was in bondage to destructive things contrary to the Word of God. A bondage can be described as a slavery or captivity, imprisonment, and a restraint of a person's liberty by compulsion. These negative bondages affected her finances, and these bondages will affect ours, too if they are not overcome.

Another way to look at a financial bondage is to

compare it to a yoke. A good example of a yoke is where they put two oxen heads together in a heavy wooden frame. What we are yoked to will determine our destiny in life. If we are yoked to the Word of God, it gets rid of all the bondages. We will delve into identifying various types of bondages and how to be free from them in the following chapters. For now, let's focus on the heart first because that is where lasting freedom comes from.

Remember, financial freedom begins in your heart, not your bank account. Our attitude or aroma toward finances reflects our attitude toward God and His Word.

Attitude of Your Heart

Some Christian movies can facilitate powerful learning experiences through drama. The movie "Facing the Giants" by the Kendrick brothers, is one that comes to my mind. Many scenes in the movie depict giants of fear and failure that can loom in our hearts. And we are the ones with the mighty power to overcome these giants and experience victory over them. The movie depicts a dramatic scene where Brock, the leader of the football team, responds negatively to a comment made by the coach about his confidence in winning against an opposing team. In the game of football, the leader is extremely influential over the other players on the team. In the movie, Brock had a bad attitude, and the coach called him on it.

The head coach said, "Your attitude is like the aroma of your heart. If your attitude stinks, it means your heart is not right. How's your attitude, Brock?" The assistant coach walked over to the young man and pretended like he was sniffing his attitude with his nose. When the head coach asked the young leader if he thought the team was going to do well in the upcoming game, Brock responded with a lack of confidence and excuses. The head coach countered with a call-to-action statement and said, "Then you'll be ok with the 'death crawl?' And give me your absolute best!" All the remaining team members groaned loudly at the thought of doing the physically demanding 'death crawl.' The coach continued saying, "Give me your best." Then he blindfolded Brock because he didn't want him to see where he was going or to give up when he thought he couldn't go any further.

The 'death crawl' required Brock to walk on all fours on the football field with a fellow teammate on his back. Since he was starting on the beginning yard line, he asked the head coach how far he wanted him to go, "To the 20-yard line?" As the young man started crawling from the first-yard line of the football field with his teammate on his back, the head coach kept encouraging him along the way. He answered, "You keep going until you can't go anymore, then we'll see."

The coach kept motivating him along his difficult journey of crawling on the field, "Don't stop!... Don't quit 'til you have nothing left!... Keep going!... Give me your very best! ...Give me your very best!... Don't quit 'til you have nothing left!... Don't give up!... Keep going!... Give me more!... Don't quit!... Don't quit!... Keep going!... Don't quit! ... Give me more!... You can do it!... Don't quit!"

Brock groaned loudly after a while and said, "It hurts!" Then, the head coach quickly knelt on his hands and knees alongside him and yelled, "You can do it!... Don't quit!... Don't quit!... Don't quit!"

This was an intense time! The remainder of the team, who were on the sidelines, stood up in amazement to watch how far their team leader was going to crawl with this physically intense 'death crawl' and their coach repeatedly yelling, "Don't quit!"

The moment arrived when the young athlete reached the end of his strength and physically collapsed from exhaustion on the football field, with drops of sweat pouring off his face. He did not know how far he had gone. When the coach took the blindfold off his face, he told him to look up. At that moment, the young man realized he had crawled the entire length of the football field with a 160-pound teammate on his back and was now in the End Zone. What a powerful demonstration of perseverance!

The head coach used this example as a learning opportunity for the young team leader. He said, "You are the most influential person on this team. If you walk around defeated, the rest of the team will, too!" After this impactful exercise, the young man immediately changed his attitude and recognized the strength that was inside him. As a result, the whole team's attitude changed for the positive, and they began winning football games during the season.

As the leader of our home, our attitude toward finances is going to direct the attitude of our entire household. Remember, financial freedom begins in our hearts, not our bank accounts. Our heart is the ruling center of our whole person. It springs forth all the desires in our life. Our heart is seen as the seat of our affections – our mind, will, and emotions. Our heart affects our thoughts, our speech, and our actions – good or bad. An appropriate question to ask ourselves is, "What is in my heart?"

Guard Your Heart

Would you leave your car doors unlocked while you park your car in a crime-ridden area of town? Would you leave your house unlocked all day long while you go to work? Most people wouldn't. Why? It is wisdom to protect the valuable things entrusted to us during our lifetime, whether they be material possessions or relationships. That is why people lock their car doors or their homes when they are away from them. They want to stop any temptation by an enemy to steal, kill, and destroy their goods or precious loved ones, for that matter.

Since financial freedom begins in our hearts, it would be a wise decision to protect our hearts with the same diligence we would protect our material possessions. Genesis 2:15 says, "Then the Lord God took the man and put him in the garden of Eden to tend and keep it." The word tend means to cultivate and the word keep means to guard.

Keep your heart with all diligence.

The garden was Adam's responsibility. Today, we don't have a perfect physical Garden of Eden where God abides. Now we have God living on the inside of our spirit man, if we have invited Him into our hearts to be our Lord and Savior. If you haven't received Jesus into your heart, you are welcome to do so. Please see the Prayer for Salvation and Baptism of the Holy Spirit at the end of this book.

We could consider our hearts to be a modern-day Garden of Eden. Just like Adam was given the responsibility to tend and keep the Garden, our responsibility is to tend and <u>keep</u> our hearts. The Hebrew word for <u>keep</u> is *Shamar*, which means to hedge about, to guard, or to protect.

Potentially, we have a beautiful spiritual garden in our hearts. The heart is the seat of our affections and our personality. Have you ever heard money described as taking on someone's personality? It does. By itself, money is neither good nor bad. However, money takes on the personality of the person who has control of it and reveals the attitude of their hearts when they spend it.

Proverbs 4:23 says, "Keep your heart with all diligence, for out of it spring the issues of life." Matthew 12:35 says, "A good man out of the good treasure of his heart brings forth good things, and an evil man out of the evil treasure brings forth evil things."

There was an old TV commercial enticing people to use a credit card, and their famous question to the viewing audience was, "What is in your wallet?" Here are some powerful questions we can ask ourselves: "Am I stingy or generous?" "Am I selfish or compassionate?" "Am I angry or loving?" "Am I full of fear or faith?"

The question only you can answer is, "What is in your heart?"

The Principle of Generosity

The smell of freshly baked brownies filled the house. Ten-year-old Johnny followed the fresh aroma and ran into the kitchen along with his neighborhood buddies. He was looking forward to eating some delicious brownies and sharing them with his friends. They had been playing outdoors for hours and were hungry for a good snack. But this time, Johnny was disappointed with this mom when she rationed only one small brownie for each boy out of the abundance of brownies he saw in the pans. He knew it was not about the sugar content but more about a poverty mindset as this mom used to follow a rationing procedure with other things as well. Perhaps growing up during the Depression in the 1930s had a negative impact on her outlook. From Johnnie's perspective, he felt like he and his friends were insignificant, and their desires were not considered.

Johnny had fond memories of the time he was over at his neighborhood friend's house, and his friend's mom made a big tray of lemon meringue cupcakes. She told the boys they could have as many cupcakes as they wanted. Of course, the desserts were so filling that each boy could only eat two. He remembers there was an attitude of generosity that made him feel welcomed, valued, and even loved. What a difference a generous heart makes.

Then came the marvelous day when Johnny's mom changed her attitude to one of generosity. What happened? Her freezer unexpectedly lost electricity after she had just stocked up on several half gallons of ice cream on sale and put them in the freezer. They were all going to go to waste if someone didn't eat them quickly. Mom turned to her son and asked, "Johnny, would you please call all your friends in the neighborhood and invite them to come over to eat as much ice cream as they want?"

It's the truth that we know, apply, and put into practice that will make us free.

All the neighborhood boys came over and received a big spoon and a half gallon of ice cream each. The boys would rotate swimming in the above-ground pool and eating some more ice cream in between swims. Do you want to know something amazing? None of the boys remembered the time when this mom was stingy with the brownies. They all remembered her generous nature with the ice cream invitation. They had fun that day, and it fostered a memory that would mark them in their hearts for the rest of their lives.

Can you think of a time when you were the recipient of someone else's generosity? How did it make you feel?

God is a generous God, and it is important for us to see Him that way, too.

When we put into practice the biblical truths God has laid out in His Word, we can experience this freedom in our hearts. We shall know the truth, and the truth shall make us free. It's the truth that we know, apply, and put into practice that will make us free.

Like the mom with the ice cream dilemma...she could have thrown all the half-gallon containers away instead of blessing the boys with them. But she chose to apply the kingdom principle of generosity and invited all the neighborhood boys over to enjoy the treat.

And what does all this have to do with finances?

Plenty! Because if our hearts are free, then we are no longer in bondage. We are free to give. We are free to receive. We are free to manage all the goodness that we receive. And finally, we are free to love God, partner with Him, and help others by going beyond ourselves and expanding God's Kingdom on this earth.

Freedom Is About Choices

Suddenly, the phone rang, and it startled me. "Who could be calling me this late in the day?" I asked myself. I was just about to pack up my things and leave the office when I decided to answer this last phone call with the unrecognizable number on the Caller ID. To my surprise, it was Bill and Holly on the other end of the phone. I stumbled over my words when I asked them, "What can I do for you?" The last time I saw them was when they left my office in distress to talk privately and discuss the significant loss that was revealed to them through our financial discovery process.

I waited for a response. Bill's voice was shaking a bit when he asked if he and Holly could come back into my office to continue their financial planning journey. From our previous conversation, Bill said they realized that financial freedom was not all about money. He and Holly saw that financial freedom really does begin in their hearts first. They recognized they had some financial bondages common to all of us in their hearts that needed to be dealt with first before they could be successful in life. And they were ready to embrace the journey no matter what it required. I was ecstatic when I heard their quality decision to be financially free.

Join us along this financial journey. We are going to defeat the ugly giants of insecurity, fear, anxiety, ungratefulness, enslavement, envy, bitterness, and disillusionment that loom in our hearts. These enemies have tormented us long enough. No more! We are pressing on to learn the truth and apply it to our situations, using the spiritual weapons in the Word of God and learning to live a prosperous life by faith.

God's Thoughts for Your Journey

Here are some powerful kingdom thoughts to meditate on and let sink deep into your heart. They have the power to bring victory into your life and finances.

"This Book of the Law shall not depart from your mouth, but you shall meditate in it day and night, that you may observe to do according to all that is written in it. For then you will make your way prosperous, and then you will have good success." (Joshua 1:8)

"Counsel is mine, and sound wisdom; I am understanding, I have strength." (Proverbs 8:14)

"Brethren, I do not count myself to have apprehended; but one thing I do, forgetting those things which are behind and reaching forward to those things which are ahead." (Philippians 3.13)

Chapter 2

Is Insecurity Secretly Ruining Your Life?

Have you ever heard yourself say, "Lord, how do I get rid of all these insecurities hiding in my heart? They are masquerading themselves as unconquerable giants, intimidating me and preventing me from obtaining the promises of God and appropriating them in my life. And, of course, there is not just one culprit, but numerous giants in the land God promised me. Please help me overcome them!"

The good news is they can be overcome with faith in God and acting on His Word. We are not to be afraid of them. I like what the Scripture says in Numbers 14:6-9.

> *But Joshua the son of Nun and Caleb the son of Jephunneh, who were among those who had spied out the land, tore their clothes;*

and they spoke to all the congregation of the children of Israel, saying: "The land we passed through to spy out is an exceedingly good land. If the Lord delights in us, then He will bring us into this land and give it to us 'a land which flows with milk and honey.' Only do not rebel against the Lord, nor fear the people of the land, for they are our bread; their protection has departed from them, and the Lord is with us. Do not fear them. (Numbers 14:6-9)

We are not to rebel against the LORD nor fear the people of the land, as our enemies are bread for us. Since their protection is gone from them, they can be conquered with spiritual weapons.

When I was in my 30s, it's been too many years ago. At this point, I lost a lot of material things simultaneously, and the life I was comfortable with ended in disaster. I experienced a divorce, lost my husband and marital status of 10 years, and half the earthly possessions I worked so hard to accumulate. Also, I lost all my worldly friends, who were the married couples my former husband and I associated with. They just disappeared and abandoned us. Then, I was laid off from my job along with many others in a billion-dollar corporation's third downsizing and lost my high-paying management income. All this happened right after I received Jesus as the Lord and Savior of my life.

There was very little so-called "honeymoon" in my newfound relationship with Jesus. I immediately experienced spiritual warfare in my life. My circumstances did not make me feel very secure at this time in my life. But I clung to a hope in God that things would change for the better someday...and eventually, they did.

God wants us to place our total trust and confidence in Him.

Many people struggle with insecurity. As a Christian, I've found that if we are not rooted and grounded in our identity in Christ, then we are going to be unstable when either the people, the position, or the possessions we previously had get removed from our lives. It takes time to develop maturity in the Lord by the process of renewing our minds to agree with the Word of God. My encouragement to all of us is to be patient with ourselves during this growth process and learn to lean on God's grace.

What is insecurity? A want of safety. Or a want of confidence in safety. Insecurity is the result of putting your confidence in people, positions, or possessions that can be unstable and can be easily taken from you.

God wants us to place our total trust and confidence in Him. It takes time to develop a deep trust in God. It just doesn't happen overnight. Proverbs

3:5 says, "Trust in the Lord with all your heart and lean not on your own understanding."

There are many sources of insecurity. The common denominator among them all is simply a lack of trust in God. Let me give you an example. Have you ever asked someone, "What do you do for a living?" And many times, their answer is going to be, "I am...a bookkeeper," or "I am...an engineer," or "I am...a manager of whatever." They are using the words "I am." What if they said, "I work as...a bookkeeper. I work as ...an engineer." When we use the words "I am," we identify with something other than what the Word of God says we are. We yoke ourselves to something else—the position or the possession—that is temporary, unstable, or insecure.

You may think I'm getting too detailed here; however, it's important to understand that our true identity is in Jesus. Many times, we subconsciously identify with unstable factors—people, positions, or possessions—but they are not our identity. God's Word is the mirror we are to look at to tell us the true nature of who we are in Christ.

Can you identify any areas in your life that you are clinging to for security today?

The Proverbs 31 Woman

Although it was a cold winter afternoon in Massachusetts, the denominational church building I was in was nice and warm and filled with attentive women who were eager to hear our guest speaker, the presbytery's wife. I listened attentively as she was an older woman in a position of authority in the church I attended, and she had biblical knowledge. After all, I thought, "This important leader was invited to our ladies' meeting, so she must have something meaningful to say to us."

I will always remember this. She was teaching us the Bible from the passage in Proverbs 31 about the virtuous woman. She said, "You can't really be the Proverbs 31 woman." I heard all the other words of unbelief conveyed in her message about a Proverbs 31 woman being unattainable! Unattainable? In my mind, I was thinking, "Oh no! Wait a minute! I just left everything from the world behind to hook up with the Jesus in the Bible and to be what He said I could be, and now you're telling me I can't be a Proverbs 31 woman because it's not possible for me to attain? This description of a Proverbs 31 woman must be true—it's in the Bible, isn't it? I left my past behind to be what Jesus said I could be in my future. It must be true!"

I had to decide right then and there what I was going to believe in my heart—the Bible or her unbelief. I decided to believe what the Word of God said because that was the truth, and it gave me hope to believe for something better in my broken life. The Bible was my anchor. This was an important decision that would affect the rest of my life. I could not take what she said to be the absolute truth because it did not line up with what was written in the Word of God. In her defense, maybe she misunderstood that to become a Proverbs 31 woman, we must be perfect in the natural, and that is not humanly possible.

What I believe the Proverbs 31 virtuous woman means is that we live a life of purpose, diligence, forgiveness, and repentance. We don't have to be perfect through striving with our own self-efforts but rather choose to follow Scriptural guidelines and draw on the strength of the perfect person of Jesus, who is living on the inside of us, to lead and guide us in this process of transformation.

When I lived in Massachusetts, I had a mentor friend who told me I could speak the Word of God over myself, like washing myself with the water of the Word. I liked that idea because I was single at the time and did not have a husband who could wash me, as his wife, with the water of the Word like it says in Ephesians 5:25-26, "Husbands, love your wives, just as Christ also loved the church and gave Himself for her, that He might sanctify and cleanse her with the washing of water by the word."

I made a quality decision to take the verses in Proverbs 31:10-31 and recite them over myself. I asked, "How am I going to do this?" My mentor suggested I speak the Word over myself while I was in the shower. I agreed that it was a great idea. So, I memorized Proverbs 31, verses 10-31, and began reciting them over myself regularly while in the shower, and I still do this practice today.

I took the suggestion of my mentor friend and found one way to combat insecurity by speaking the Word of God over myself and believing it to be true for me. I began to anchor myself in the Word of God. Now, that didn't mean the enemy didn't try to come and steal the Word of God out of my heart. Believe me, he tried daily! That's his job – to steal, kill, and destroy. And when I inadvertently let the enemy steal the Word out of my heart because of my ignorance, I just continued redepositing the Word in my heart. I made the decision to yoke myself to Jesus no matter how many lies the enemy throws my way.

Yoking ourselves to the Word of God will help to eliminate insecurity. Be alert, as there can be other hidden dark areas in our hearts that may arise after insecurity is dealt with and need to be conquered with the Word of God.

My questions for you to ponder are, "Who are you yoked to?" "What are you yoked to?"

God is not going to automatically remove all those other hidden bondages in our hearts that He knows we are yoked to until we admit they have been taking up priority in our lives over the Word of God. We may not even realize we are yoked to unstable things until they are taken away from us.

Partnering with God

At this point, you may be thinking, "What does all this have to do with finances?" A lot, actually! Everything! Deuteronomy 8:18 says, "And you shall remember the Lord your God, for it is He who gives you power to get wealth, that He may establish His covenant which He swore to your fathers, as it is this day." God is not going to rain money down from heaven. He has already given us the power to get wealth. Where is that power? It is coming from inside of us. It is flowing from our hearts. Financial freedom begins in our hearts, not our bank accounts.

The Lord always gives us money with a mission and prosperity with a purpose. He blesses us so that we can be a blessing to others. The insecurity that is lurking in the deep recesses of our souls can hinder our prosperity.

If you are insecure, ask yourself, "What am I focusing on?" "Am I trying to protect myself?" We will not be focusing on working with God to advance His Kingdom if we are worried about protecting and providing for ourselves because we are insecure. God needs His people to be secure in Him, to listen to His voice, trust Him, and do what He says. God has assignments for us to accomplish here on this earth.

Imagine what our lives would be like if we could personally, in one day, serve breakfast to 35 orphan girls in Guatemala and, at the same time, pay for a single mom's opportunity to take nursing courses to better her life in Wyoming, while also flipping the switch on the auditorium lights for a pastor and his wife to preach the gospel to the locals in Belize. How could we do all these projects at the same time? We are not omnipresent. However, we could use our discretionary money to partner with God and accomplish great things like these and so much more while never leaving our hometown.

God has assignments for us to accomplish here on this earth.

What is missing from your life?

- A biblical purpose for wealth.
- The financial freedom to make a difference in the world.
- The reward that comes from partnering with God.

If any of these things are missing from your life, there is hope for you.

Insecurity Defeated

Bill and Holly came eagerly to my office to reconvene their discussions about finances. They made the quality decision to be financially free. They were ready to embrace the Word of God and do things God's way.

Their serene faces revealed a quiet peace that was present in their countenances. They made peace with God and with one another. How refreshing it was to work with them in planning their financial affairs this time we met. We worked through their budget together and identified areas where they could reduce expenses and save more money toward their future family goals. They were in one mind and had one purpose. In a marriage, unity between a husband and wife and agreement together with the Word of God, are keys to success and increase in their lives.

How did they reach such peace? To be honest with you, it was simple yet very challenging. Holly's insecurities were revealed in their financial condition on the first visit when we met. Once these weaknesses were discovered, Holly admitted them, repented, and willingly made the quality decision to seek God's help and change. She sought godly counsel and chose God's best and His way of security. Once she changed her heart, victory followed, and their finances began to increase supernaturally.

The Holy Spirit and the Word of God are our best teachers for seeing from a different vantage point how to prosper on this earth. Bill and Holly experienced for themselves that financial freedom begins in their hearts, not their bank accounts.

Be encouraged to stay on this journey of faith with us and not lose heart. "And let us not grow weary while doing good, for in due season we shall reap if we do not lose heart." (Galatians 6:9)

We are now moving forward to conquer another financial bondage with the Word of God called fear!

God's Thoughts for Your Journey

Here are some powerful kingdom thoughts to meditate on and let them sink deep into your heart. They have the power to bring victory into your life and finances.

"He who dwells in the secret place of the Most High Shall abide under the shadow of the Almighty. I will say of the LORD, "He is my refuge and my fortress; My God, in Him I will trust." (Psalm 91:1-2)

"Therefore do not cast away your confidence, which has great reward." (Hebrews 10:35)

"Beloved, I pray that you may prosper in all things and be in health, just as your soul prospers." (3 John 2)

Chapter 3

We Have All Felt Fear

We've all felt fear. Heart pounding. Palms sweating and struggling to breathe through a tight throat. Eyes darting for a way out. Fear is real, and it can be a yoke in our lives, preventing us from experiencing total freedom in our hearts and finances. Fear is an enemy of faith. It contradicts the Word of God. "For God has not given us a spirit of fear, but of power and of love and of a sound mind." (2 Timothy 1:7).

I was amazed to discover the number of times the words "fear not" appear in the New King James Version of the Bible—150 times! Jesus is serious about the bold stand He wants us to take against our enemy. In fact, "fear not" is a command and not a suggestion for debate. Fear is a weapon from the devil that will destroy our faith if we let it.

Without faith, it is impossible to please God. If the

enemy can stop our faith, then he can hinder God's plan for our lives and possibly the lives of others. "But without faith it is impossible to please Him, for he who comes to God must believe that He is, and that He is a rewarder of those who diligently seek Him." (Hebrews 11:6).

Whatever bondage we are yoked to will have the biggest influence in our lives.

As believers in Christ, we are not just ordinary people but children of the Most High God. He has equipped us with His power to be victorious. How? He has given us the Spirit of adoption so we can overcome fear as a child of God. "For you did not receive the spirit of bondage again to fear, but you received the Spirit of adoption by whom we cry out, "Abba, Father." (Romans 8:15). The spirit of God enables us to overcome whatever adversity or trouble presents itself against us.

Whatever bondage we are yoked to will have the biggest influence in our lives. If we are yoked to fear, we will experience intense, unpleasant emotions in response to perceiving or recognizing danger or threat. Fear is everywhere in this world. The enemy attacks us with his spirit of fear through his lies on television, newspapers, magazines, social media, politics, man-made religion, movies, etc. Satan uses fear as a weapon to disrupt our faith.

It is imperative for us to be yoked to Jesus, the Word of God, the Solid Rock, the One Who never changes, and not to be yoked to fear if we want to be victorious in this life and with our finances.

What is the definition of fear? It is the painful apprehension of some impending evil. Fear happens when we dwell upon losing all the temporal things that we put our trust and alliance on. Fear is a very real spiritual force. It is not fictitious; it is real. However, be encouraged because the light of God's Word is so much greater.

The Light

As I sat relaxing in my comfortable chair one sunny morning, I had a vivid dream that I was in a room full of darkness with a shovel in my hand. I was toiling, struggling, and striving to shovel the darkness out—shoveling and shoveling and shoveling. Do you remember what I said about fear? Fear is a very real spiritual force. I was trying to shovel out this darkness, and after a long time, I was getting very tired and realized nothing was happening. All my efforts to shovel out the darkness were fruitless. The darkness and fear were still there in the room.

Then suddenly, I heard this voice in a Texas accent twang say, "Whatcha doin'?" And I recognized that unique voice behind me. It was the voice of a godly minister. I had been to his Bible college and worked in his ministry, so I was familiar with his distinct southern-accented voice. I didn't see him in the dream; I only heard his voice. The next thing I knew was that he effortlessly shined a little light on the situation, like with a flashlight. And guess what? All the darkness instantly left and then the dream ended.

Where there is light, darkness cannot exist. At that moment I knew what the answer was for me—it was to stop trying to get rid of the darkness in my life but rather to focus on the light. Jesus said that He was the light of the world. "Then Jesus spoke to them again, saying, "I am the light of the world. He who follows Me shall not walk in darkness, but have the light of life." (John 8:12).

How many times do we struggle and try to get rid of our faults and fears by focusing on them? I found out that it doesn't work. Instead of focusing on the darkness, my fault, or the problem, what I knew at that moment was to focus on the Word of God, which is the answer. Focusing on the light and on everything that is good and right will overcome the darkness. Light is always the solution to remove the darkness. Then, the fear will disappear from our hearts. God is light. "This is the message which we have heard from Him and declare to you, that God is light and in Him is no darkness at all." (1 John 1:5).

Although the fear may disappear from our hearts,

it does not disappear from this world and will reappear in other situations or problems. It is still here in the physical realm. As a result, we need to learn how NOT to cooperate with it next time it raises its ugly head. We can soar above every fear when we learn to live by faith in God's Word.

Remember, fear is a very real spiritual force that comes from the enemy. When we refuse to cooperate with the enemy and his fear tactics and walk by faith instead, he no longer has any power over us. We can choose to walk in the light of God's Word instead. We can choose to live in freedom. In my God-given dream, with the shovel in my hand, all I needed to do was to turn the light on, and the darkness disappeared.

Of course, there will be other situations and circumstances in our lives where fear will try to rise again. The solution will always be the same—shine the light of the Word of God on the situation and watch the darkness flee.

You may be thinking, "What does all this have to do with finances?" "Plenty!" The Kingdom of God operates differently than the world system. If we want to succeed and thrive in life, we must follow our heavenly Father's example. First, God gave His only begotten Son, and then He received His heart's desire—sons and daughters to love and fellowship with. "For God so loved the world that He gave His only begotten Son, that whoever believes in Him should not perish but have everlasting life." (John 3:16). He first gave, and then He received something valuable in return.

God's Love

Spiritual light in the Word of God comes from the source of love. God is love. Knowing God's love for us personally can eliminate fear in our hearts. 1 John 4:18 says, "There is no fear in love; but perfect love casts out fear, because fear involves torment. But he who fears has not been made perfect in love."

This does not mean we have to strive to be perfect or even have perfect love for God. God is the only one who is perfect. It means when we believe in how much God loves us, we can stop striving and forget about all the things we are afraid of. Now, I know this may sound simple, but I also understand it may not be easy to do. It will require diligence to cast down all our negative thoughts and renew our minds to the Word of God. The good news is that it is doable because God said it.

Religion is man's best attempt to try to please and love God. We may have thoughts that say, "I've got to do this, and if I do that, then God will be pleased with me and love me." Those legalistic thoughts are full of self effort and constant striving. That thinking process is tormenting because God's love cannot be attained that way. Grace, on the other hand, facilitates a personal relationship with God by simply receiving His unconditional love for us personally, just because He loves us. Jesus has already paid the price of redemption for us to be able to fellowship with God, our Father, and receive His love freely. Love is a gift from God.

When we believe the magnitude of God's love for us, we will not let fear rule over us.

Love thinks of others first. Let's be real. We all want our needs met, too. In the Kingdom of God, our needs are met by helping others. Love learns how to rise above a suffered wrong. It's not denying the unjust situation never happened. It's that love rises above it. Love believes the best of every person even when it is difficult in the natural to do so. Love always has hope. Love is strong. If we feel ourselves getting weak, we may need to check our love walk. "Therefore, be imitators of God as dear children. And walk in love, as Christ also has loved us and given Himself for us, an offering and a sacrifice to God for a sweet-smelling aroma." (Ephesians 5:1-2).

Love never fails, and when you walk in love, you will never fail either.

Stewardship

God is love, and His nature is a generous giver. I want to share this incredible story with you:

"How did you raise $3 million dollars for the benefit of others with one charitable event?" I asked my wealthy client, Edward, as he sat across from me in my office. I was curious to hear his backstory. Edward was a burly gentleman, successful businessman, speaker, and former pastor. He sat quietly for a moment, thinking intently, and then he focused on me, had a twinkle in his eyes, and smiled. With that look on his face, I knew I was about to hear an incredible story.

He began to tell me that early on in his career as a young pastor in a denominational church, how he wrote a unique and powerful stewardship class. When he taught the material to his congregation, church attendance and finances substantially increased. News of Edward's success eventually reached the corporate level. Now other pastors in his denomination were beginning to hear about his tremendous church growth. Then Edward was asked a question he was not prepared to answer.

The other pastors requested a copy of his

extensive stewardship class notes. They wanted to know what he taught that was so effective in every area, including the increase of finances in his church. Then he paused, looked down at the floor, admitted his initial area of weakness to me, and said, "At first, I didn't want to give it to them." He admitted he wanted to be at the top of his denomination and didn't want to share his secret of success with anyone else. He was afraid if he told the others, they would advance ahead of him and be higher up in the denomination.

A few months passed, the seasons changed, and God softened his heart. Edward loved the Lord and wanted to please Him more than anything else. So, he changed his mind, desired to be generous, and shared his stewardship information with the others. He even made multiple copies of his notes and distributed them to everyone without holding anything back. He got rid of his selfish, fleshly tendency nagging at his heart and the fear of not being successful or rising to the top of his denomination. After he changed his attitude, he was now free from that fear.

Edward said if he had not made that change of heart, conquered the fear, and chose generosity early on in his career, he would never have been able to have his successful organization today that could raise $3 million dollars in one event. God showed him that his humility and generosity opened the door for him to be where he is today. How would God be able to trust him with $3 million dollars if he was unable to share his little notes on stewardship with the other people at the beginning of his career?

The good news is that we have the same choice. We can choose humility and generosity or prideful and selfishness.

What choice are you going to make?

The Decision

Many years ago, I attended a business conference, paid a considerable amount of my own money to register, used my personal time off from work, and took numerous pages of precious notes from the keynote speakers. Although every employee in the corporation was given the same opportunity, some chose not to attend. When I returned to the office from the conference, I was so excited about the awesome experience I had and wanted to share my enthusiasm with the others who chose not to attend.

The best way I knew to share my excitement was to offer my precious notes to anyone who did not attend but wanted a copy. There was no hesitation in me, as my heart was filled with joy. I appreciated the opportunity to photocopy all my notes and bless them, and I prayed that they would receive many revelations from my notes, too.

What is God asking you to share with others from your heart? Remember, financial freedom begins in your heart, not your bank account.

Overcoming Fear

Let's take a few minutes to sit quietly and ask ourselves what fears are holding us back in our hearts from following God's will for our lives.

Are we afraid of:

- Being rejected by others
- Failing
- Doing something wrong
- SuccessBeing left behind
- Not being able to get a good job
- Being criticized
- Shame
- Public speaking
- Getting sick
- Lack - Not having enough money to pay our bills

You may be thinking, "How do I get rid of the fear

that is tormenting me?" The answer is to shine the light on it. We cannot shine the light in a dark room unless we first take action to enter the dark room and face our giant of fear.

Humility is admitting our fear and bringing it to the light. If our fear problem remains hidden, it is still in darkness, and our freedom will be hindered. Once we admit our fear, we can cast the care of it over on the Lord and not worry about it anymore. "Therefore humble yourselves under the mighty hand of God, that He may exalt you in due time, casting all your care upon Him, for He cares for you." (1 Peter 5:6-7)

Now is the time to fill our hearts with the light of the Word of God. We can dig in, read it, and meditate on biblical verses that apply to our specific situation. Love never fails. We cannot overdose on the love of God. He is always faithful. The following prayer in Ephesians 3:14-20 is a great Scripture for us to meditate on.

For this reason I bow my knees to the Father of our Lord Jesus Christ, from whom the whole family in heaven and earth is named, that He would grant you, according to the riches of His glory, to be strengthened with might through His Spirit in the inner man, that Christ may dwell in your hearts through faith; that you, being rooted and grounded in love, may be able to comprehend with all the saints what is the width and length and depth and height— to know the love of Christ which passes knowledge; that you may be filled with all the fullness of God. Now to Him who is able to do exceedingly abundantly above all that we ask or think, according to the power that works in us. (Ephesians 3:14-20)

Now is the time to fill our hearts with the light of the Word of God.

Another way to overcome fear is to build up our faith in God's love for us. 1 John 4:18 says, "There is no fear in love; but perfect love casts out fear, because fear involves torment. But he who fears has not been made perfect in love." This means that when we believe in how much God loves us, eventually, we will stop striving and forget about all the things we are afraid of. I know this sounds so simple, but it takes diligence.

We can overcome fear because God, who is in us, is greater than the enemy that is in the world. "You are of God, little children, and have overcome them because He who is in you is greater than he who is in the world." (1 John 4:4)

And what does all this have to do with finances? Plenty! Because if our hearts are free, we are no longer in bondage. We are free to give. We are free to receive. We are free to manage all this goodness that we receive. And finally, we are free to love God, partner with Him, and help others by going beyond ourselves and expanding God's Kingdom on this earth.

Fear was one of the many financial bondages Bill and Holly conquered in their lives. Today, it is so refreshing to see them experience the financial freedom they had desired in their hearts all along but were unable to accomplish alone before they began this journey.

Thank you for continuing with us on this journey. Remember, financial freedom begins in your heart, not your bank account.

Some of you want to get right to "the money part." However, we must lay a solid foundation before we can build a godly financial future.

For example, when we build a house, we begin with a blueprint before the homesite is prepared. Next, we pour the foundation and sequentially add the framing, plumbing, electrical, etc. If your financial house is not built on the solid foundation of the Word of God, it will collapse during the storms of life.

> *Everyone then who hears these words of mine and does them will be like a wise man who built his house on the rock. And the rain fell, and the floods came, and the winds blew and beat on that house, but it did not fall, because it had been founded on the rock. And everyone who hears these words of mine and does not*

*do them will be like a foolish man who built
his house on the sand. And the rain fell, and
the floods came, and the winds blew and beat
against that house, and it fell, and great was
the fall of it. (Matthew 7:24-27 ESV)*

We are gaining inner strength and are ready to
move forward and defeat another financial bondage
with the Word of God. This giant is called anxiety!

God's Thoughts for Your Journey

Here are some powerful kingdom thoughts to
meditate on and let them sink deep into your heart.
They have the power to bring victory into your life
and finances.

"In righteousness you shall be established; You
shall be far from oppression, for you shall not fear;
And from terror, for it shall not come near you.
Indeed, they shall surely assemble, but not because
of Me. Whoever assembles against you shall fall for
your sake." (Isaiah 54:14-15)

"For God has not given us a spirit of fear, but of

power and of love and of a sound mind." (2 Timothy 1:7)

"But without faith it is impossible to please Him, for he who comes to God must believe that He is, and that He is a rewarder of those who diligently seek Him." (Hebrews 11:6)

Chapter 4

Be Anxious for Nothing

"Why are you crying?" I asked Lisa as she sat nervously in my office, fidgeting in her seat, tears streaming down her cheeks. Lisa was a single mom who recently gave birth to her first baby. Her parents referred her to me because they knew Lisa needed financial guidance, wisdom, and direction for her life and for her newborn baby. She was starting her life over again—both in Christ and in her financial affairs as a single mom.

Lisa was filled with anxiety about her future. What was she going to do with her life? How would she be able to take care of her newborn daughter financially? These and many other concerns were overwhelming to Lisa. Anxiety can be described as a concern representing some event, future or uncertain, which disturbs the mind and keeps it in a state of painful uneasiness. Anxiety is the emotion that results when we worry about problems, especially financial ones, instead of casting our cares upon the Lord. "Casting all your care upon Him, for He cares for you." (1 Peter 5:7)

After reviewing Lisa's financial situation, bringing her current circumstances to light, and developing an organized plan of action for her to follow, Lisa smiled, her tears disappeared, and she saw a renewed hope for her financial future. Now, she was better equipped to move forward. The financial bondage or yoke of anxiety that was preventing her from experiencing freedom in her finances was no longer a threat.

Writing things down and organizing our financial position is an excellent way to bring a hidden vision to light and ignite hope for the future. How can we see a solution to a problem or situation if we don't know what it looks like? Putting our facts and thoughts in writing helps us focus. Our brains are also meant for fostering creative ideas, not just for storing data.

After the facts of the situation are revealed, the next step is to seek God's wisdom on how to solve it. The book of Proverbs provides great insight into how to live our lives successfully. "Wisdom is the principal thing; Therefore get wisdom. And in all your getting, get understanding." (Proverbs 4:7)

You may consider asking yourself these questions:

"Have I fallen victim to worrisome thoughts?" "Is anxiety racing in my heart and choking out my financial prosperity?" Our honest answers to these questions will benefit us in finding the appropriate solution and moving forward in our lives.

When potential clients walk through the door of my office, they have issues that require answers, and they are looking to me and my team for solutions. Just because they have issues doesn't mean they have to embrace the bondage of anxiety to go along with them. However, in many cases, these people demonstrate worrisome thoughts and behaviors, as in Lisa's case.

There are many problems in life that could produce anxiety. Here are a few:

- You can't see how to buy a newer vehicle to replace the old one that keeps breaking down.
- You're frustrated about needing to buy a bigger house for your growing family with limited income while feeling cramped in a small, rented place.
- You don't qualify for a loan, yet you want to start a new business.

- You're losing hope that your heart's desires and dreams will ever come to pass.

Wisdom of God

Over the years, I have found that each one of these situations has solutions that can be found by seeking the wisdom of God. I know it is easier to say, "Don't worry!" than it is to do it. God does not want us to be anxious about anything. It says in Philippians 4:6-7, "Be anxious for nothing, but in everything by prayer and supplication, with thanksgiving, let your requests be made known to God;

Be anxious for nothing.

and the peace of God, which surpasses all understanding, will guard your hearts and minds through Christ Jesus."

There are two commands in Philippians 4:6-7. "Don't be anxious" and "Make your requests known to God." The first choice is to refuse to give in to the emotion of anxiety. The second decision is to make our requests known to God.

The simple act of writing things down, as we did in Lisa's case, was the first step in organizing her finances. From there, we sought the Lord's wisdom, wrote out her prayer requests, and rolled the care of them over to the Lord. Then, God showed us the practical steps Lisa could take to answer her issues.

This process of following God's Word brought Lisa peace, and it can bring you peace in your heart, too.

Lisa is not the only person struggling with anxiety. It happens to us all when we are faced with impossible-looking situations that we are not able to find solutions to with our own limited understanding. Of course, we are learning that we do not have to yield to this stressful emotion at all. It is our choice.

Anxiety was a bondage for me too. Worry seemed to run in my family, and I had a lot of practice with it over the years. I used to think I was being irresponsible if I didn't worry. I used to think, "It's so easy for someone else to say to me, 'Don't worry' as they are not facing my dilemma." Then I realized that if the Word of God says not to be anxious about anything, then the power to accomplish that command must be in the Word of God. I am learning to trust Jesus instead of leaning on my own understanding. The more I trust in the Lord, the more peace I have in my heart.

Renewing Our Mind

As a believer in Jesus Christ, I am constantly renewing my mind to trust God's Word and to take every thought captive to the obedience of Christ. "Casting down arguments and every high thing that exalts itself against the knowledge of God, bringing every thought into captivity to the obedience of Christ." (2 Corinthians 10:5)

When I first read 2 Corinthians 10:5 and saw that I was supposed to take every thought captive, it sounded impossible to me. How am I ever going to take every thought captive, line them up with the Word of God, and then cast down those who don't agree? I don't know about you, but I have many thoughts bombarding my mind daily. It seemed like an impossible task.

Then I remembered the day I heard an incredible story from a preacher on this subject. He said he was asked to minister to a woman in an insane asylum, and the Lord gave him the Scripture verse 2 Corinthians 10:5 to share with her. She said to him, "I can't do that. It's not possible to think on the Word of God all day long." The minister knew God would not tell us to do something without giving us the grace to follow through. Then he said, "You are already thinking about something all day long, and it is not working well for you. Why not replace your thoughts with the Word of God instead?" She agreed, and over a period, she was healed and left the insane asylum. God's Word works if it is believed and applied.

Merry-Go-Round

Have you ever felt like you were on a Merry-Go-Round with your life and finances? I was reading in Luke about the two sisters Martha and Mary. You may be familiar with their story. Martha was anxious about many things, while Mary was relaxed, sitting at the feet of Jesus and soaking in all His love and teachings. While Martha was distracted, Mary was focused on the Word of God. Notice Jesus didn't rebuke Mary, however, He gently corrected Martha. The story unfolds:

Now it happened as they went that He [Jesus] entered a certain village; and a certain woman named Martha welcomed Him into her house. And she had a sister called Mary, who also sat at Jesus' feet and heard His word. But Martha was distracted with much serving, and she approached Him and said, "Lord, do You not care that my sister has left me to serve alone? Therefore, tell her to help me." And Jesus answered and said to her, 'Martha, Martha, you are worried and troubled about many things. But one thing is needed, and

Mary has chosen that good part, which will not be taken away from her.' (Luke 10:38-42)

To get off the Merry-Go-Round...the "Martha-Go-Round"... of anxiety, distractions, and much busyness, what must we do? Cast our cares on Jesus. The Merry-Go-Round of distractions and anxious serving will always compete for our mind's attention; however, we do not have to cooperate with these destructive emotions. We can say "no" to them. It may be easier said than done, right? However, by the grace of God, we can replace the temptation to be anxious with a new habit that will yield greater rewards. We can choose the good part, as Mary did – and that is spending time in the presence of God.

This precious time with God—at Jesus' feet—is where we can cast all our cares on Him because He cares for us. Sometimes, it is very helpful to write down our anxious concerns on paper and then cast the care of them over to the Lord. He can handle them.

In our quiet time with Him, He may give us the perfect answer to our situation, an encouraging word, or show us the next step to take. In His presence, we will find our peace and comfort.

Your Heart

Financial Freedom begins in your heart, not your bank account. And if your heart is filled with anxiety and worry, your wealth will escape you. Prosperity will run away from you. The God kind of prosperity comes from peace, wisdom, and obedience—not from whirling around a merry-go-round of distractions in your mind, blasting scattered thoughts with no focused results.

The power to get wealth is within your heart.

The key to unlocking your freedom and the power to get wealth doesn't come from the outside. It comes from inside your heart. Deuteronomy 8:18 says, "And you shall remember the LORD your God, for it is He who gives you power to get wealth, that He may establish His covenant which He swore to your fathers, as it is this day."

The power to get wealth is within your heart. Praise the Lord for His faithfulness in helping you continue this journey with us. He will not let you down. "Let your character or moral disposition be free from love of money [including greed, avarice, lust, and craving for earthly possessions] and be satisfied with your present [circumstances and with what you have]; for He [God] Himself has said, I will not in any way fail you nor give you up nor leave you without support. [I will] not, [I will] not, [I will] not in any degree leave you helpless nor forsake nor let [you] down (relax My hold on you)! [Assuredly not!]" (Hebrews 13:5 AMPC)

And what does all this have to do with finances? Plenty! Because if our hearts are free, we are no longer in bondage. We are free to give. We are free to receive. We are free to manage all the goodness that we receive. And finally, we are free to love God, partner with Him, and help others by going beyond ourselves and expanding God's Kingdom on this earth.

Thank you for your steadfastness and for continuing this journey with us as we lay a solid foundation for a prosperous financial future. We are moving on to conquer another financial bondage, ungratefulness, that can hide in our hearts. Yes, we can defeat this giant, too, and be free!

God's Thoughts for Your Journey

Here are some powerful kingdom thoughts to meditate on and let them sink deep into your heart.

They have the power to bring prosperity into your life and finances.

"I would have lost heart, unless I had believed That I would see the goodness of the LORD In the land of the living. Wait on the LORD; Be of good courage, And He shall strengthen your heart; Wait, I say, on the LORD!" (Psalm 27:13-14)

"Keep your heart with all diligence, For out of it spring the issues of life. Put away from you a deceitful mouth, And put perverse lips far from you. Let your eyes look straight ahead, And your eyelids look right before you." (Proverbs 4:23-25)

"Be anxious for nothing, but in everything by prayer and supplication, with thanksgiving, let your requests be made known to God; and the peace of God, which surpasses all understanding, will guard your hearts and minds through Christ Jesus." (Philippians 4:6-7)

Chapter 5

An Attitude of Gratitude

It was a snowy winter night as I looked outside my office window, and I was secretly hoping my last financial planning appointment would be canceled due to the slippery New England Road conditions. As I waited for the phone to ring, surprisingly, my clients arrived; they decided to come despite the snowy forecast. The outside door opened slowly, and James and Kyleigh walked through the foyer, shaking the snow off their winter boots. They came earlier than their scheduled time, and I heard James announce to me in a loud voice, "Isn't the snowfall picturesque as it creates beautiful scenery clinging to the trees? We didn't know how long it would take to drive on the roads, so we left early to ensure we would arrive on time."

James and Kyleigh had been my clients for more than three years. They were serious about achieving their financial goals. James wanted to be sure his wife, Kyleigh, was taken care of with sufficient life and disability insurance coverage in the event something happened to him and he couldn't provide for his family. They were always thankful and appreciative of everything in their life—even the white snow. It was as if they didn't even consider the slippery road conditions. They were too busy focusing on the beautiful white snowfall glistening on the trees.

The lives of my clients seemed to be a great reflection of 1 Thessalonians 5:18, "In everything give thanks; for this is the will of God in Christ Jesus for you." That scripture can be misunderstood. It does not mean for us to thank God FOR the bad things that happen during our lifetime. It means to thank God IN the bad circumstances, knowing that God is the solution to turning our situations around for good.

James and Kyleigh lived their lives remembering to express gratitude on purpose for the things they had in life. They practiced their thankful attitude for years, resulting in a positive atmosphere around themselves, and it was obvious to those who knew them. They boldly shared their faith in Jesus and all He had done for them. I know I always enjoyed being around them. They brought a smile to my face.

Over the years, I've learned that constantly complaining about dire circumstances does not turn them around for the better. The more I complain, the more I attract things to complain about it.

Complaining can be difficult to escape because it's self-perpetuating. Our negative experiences feed our negative expectations, attracting new negative experiences. In other words, when we complain, we end up getting more things to complain about.

Ungratefulness

Complaining is a form of ungratefulness and can be rooted in unbelief. It is described as not being grateful or not feeling thankful for favors. Ungratefulness is a financial bondage or yoke that will prevent us from experiencing total freedom in our finances. Financial worries hinder our ability to fully appreciate and enjoy the many wonderful blessings God has already provided for us.

Complaining is a form of ungratefulness and can be rooted in unbelief.

Being ungrateful is truly a heart attitude. I heard one of my favorite ministers tell a story that marked me. The young minister had been standing in faith for years and believing God for a new automobile. Finally, the day came when someone gave him a new car—the one he had been believing God for.

When an acquaintance of his saw his new sporty vehicle, he was mesmerized by it and asked this young minister, "How did you get that car?" The minister proudly replied, "By my faith! I believed God for it!"

Later that night, God spoke up in the minister's heart and asked him, "How did you get that car I gave you?" He replied confidently, "By my faith!"

And God followed up with, "And where did you get that faith?" The minister hemmed and hawed a bit and said, "From the Word of God?"

And then God asked again, "And where did you get that Word of Mine?" Now, the minister knew he was in trouble. He said, "From Your grace?"

And finally, God asked, "And where did you get the strength to receive My grace?"

The young minister repented and said, "Oh Lord, You gave me the strength to believe Your promises. And You gave me the blessing of the car. Thank You, God. You are so good and so gracious. To You belong all the glory and the honor!"

Can you see how the young minister's response to this acquaintance, with hidden ungratefulness in his heart toward God, could have given a wrong impression of the true source of his blessing? This is quite the story of how the minister's prosperity gave his friend a false impression that he was a "big shot" man of faith and power. However, it also revealed his ungratefulness to recognize God as the true source of his blessing. To God be all the glory.

How do we get victory over this negative, ungrateful attitude? By being thankful and grateful, just like the Word of God admonishes us to be. "And let the peace that comes from Christ rule in your hearts. For as members of one body you are called to live in peace. And always be thankful." (Colossians 3:15 NLT).

My clients, James and Kyleigh, were good examples of this. They were so full of an energetic attitude of gratitude that their joy was contagious to those around them.

Grateful Leper Made Whole

A story in the Bible that comes to my mind about the power of being grateful is found in Luke 17:11-17. Ten lepers met Jesus as He was heading to Jerusalem, and they called out from a distance, "Jesus, Master, have mercy on us!" Jesus answered them, "Go, show yourselves to the priests." "As they went, they were cleansed."

And one of them, when he saw that he was healed, returned, and with a loud voice glorified God, and fell down on his face at His feet,

*giving Him thanks. And he was a Samaritan.
So Jesus answered and said, "Were there not
ten cleansed? But where are the nine? Were
there not any found who returned to give
glory to God except this foreigner?" And He
said to him, "Arise, go your way. Your faith
has made you well. (Luke 17:15-19)*

Here's the part I like the best. Jesus granted the
one grateful man, not just stopping the leprosy
from continuing to eat away his flesh but restoring
the man to complete wholeness with all his fingers
and toes!

How far do we think we'll get in life being yoked
to an ungrateful heart? Not far. And why is that?
Ungratefulness stops the supernatural flow of God's
blessings in our lives. Whereas, being grateful opens
a spiritual door to allow God to work on our behalf
and bring increase.

An ungrateful heart will "blind" us to God's goodness and the many opportunities around us. Many
times, we can't even "see" that we have a problem
in this area.

How can we recognize when we have an ungrateful attitude? We have a failure or refusal to acknowl-
edge receipt of something good from another. We
are thankless, inappreciative, and not grateful. We
complain a lot and find fault with every little thing.
We are miserable.

But praise God, we don't have to stay that way. We can change our attitude.

A Promotion

I remember many years ago when I worked at a job where I was miserable with this seemingly dead-end position. I felt so out of place, like a "fish out of water." I also saw no future there for me. I started complaining and was very ungrateful. I needed to change my heart attitude, and by the grace of God, I decided to become more thankful; after all, I did have a job. My revised decision to be grateful was like stepping into a new zone full of light and freedom.

Did my circumstances change immediately? No. But I did. The change happened inside of my heart. It was so significant that my supervisor and her manager noticed it, and they gave me a promotion and a raise! Our attitude will be felt by those around us and can be used as a tool for influencing others.

What does a grateful heart get you? In my case, it resulted in a raise and a promotion. Nine of the Lepers were healed as the disease stopped growing. The one thankful Leper was healed and made whole. All his fingers, toes, and whatever else was damaged were restored back to normal.

What can a grateful heart get you? Before you

answer that, think about your children and grand-children. When they respond thankfully to you and are excited about the gifts you've given them, doesn't their thankful attitude motivate you to want to give them more?

When we are grateful for what we do have, we begin to walk in the light of what God has already provided for us in the spirit realm. "As His divine power has given to us all things that pertain to life and godliness, through the knowledge of Him who called us by glory and virtue, by which have been given to us exceedingly great and precious promises, that through these you may be partakers of the divine nature, having escaped the corruption that is in the world through lust." (2 Peter 1:3-4)

As a result of knowing Him and walking in His light, we begin to see new opportunities, financial strategies and increases that we haven't noticed before. Remember, financial freedom begins in your heart, not your bank account.

We are building our spiritual house on the solid Rock of the Word of God.

Are you complaining, or are you grateful? The choice is yours.

Please note that we are not focusing on ourselves and digging up our past to find any bondages that may be hindering us. We are focusing on God, enjoying our personal relationship with Him, and simply asking Him if there is anything holding us back from prospering. Indeed, He will let us know when financial bondages show up in our hearts. Our responsibility is simply to listen to Him, trust, and obey.

Thank you so much for staying with us on this journey of faith. Keep your faith intact and receive your reward. "But without faith it is impossible to please Him, for he who comes to God must believe that He is, and that He is a rewarder of those who diligently seek Him." (Hebrews 11:6)

Don't quit! We are building our spiritual house on the solid Rock of the Word of God. We learn how to defeat the enslavement giant next.

God's Thoughts for Your Journey

Here are some powerful kingdom thoughts to meditate on and let them sink deep into your heart. They have the power to bring prosperity into your life and finances.

"Enter into His gates with thanksgiving, And

into His courts with praise. Be thankful to Him, and bless His name." (Psalm 100:4)

"Since we are receiving a Kingdom that is unshakable, let us be thankful and please God by worshiping him with holy fear and awe." (Hebrews 12:28 NLT)

Let All Things Praise the LORD
Praise the LORD!
Praise God in His sanctuary;
Praise Him in His mighty firmament!
Praise Him for His mighty acts;
Praise Him according to His excellent greatness!
Praise Him with the sound of the trumpet;
Praise Him with the lute and harp!
Praise Him with the timbrel and dance;
Praise Him with stringed instruments and flutes!
Praise Him with loud cymbals;
Praise Him with clashing cymbals!
Let everything that has breath praise the LORD. (PSALM 150: 1-6)

Chapter 6

No Longer Enslaved

The door opened, and I was astonished to see my client, Mr. Raymond Schmidt, walk into my office. It was a cool, crisp autumn day, and the leaves were quickly showing off their array of beautiful colors typical of the New England scenery for that season. Raymond was a WWII veteran. He was an interesting older gentleman with many life experiences from the war—some better left untold.

He was visiting his family in town for the weekend and stopped by to say hello. He was a friendly man who enjoyed conversing with others and reminiscing about the past. As he sat down, we began to chat. I enjoyed asking him questions about the war. Today was my opportunity to inquire about another subject I was curious about - the dungeons the enemy used during the war. I heard rumors over the years, but I wanted to know the truth, and I believed Raymond could tell me.

"Raymond," I said. "Would you tell me about the dungeons you saw during the WWII era? What were they like?" He looked up at the ceiling, briefly recalling the thoughts in his head, and then responded, "The dungeons were rooms or cells where the enemy held our prisoners. They were usually in a basement room, which was accessible from a hatch or hole in a high ceiling. The victims were often left to starve or dehydrate to death. These dungeons were dark, damp, and horrible." After hearing his description and seeing the look on his face, I didn't need to hear anymore.

Raymond had never been in a dungeon; however, he did help overtake the enemy camps and rescue the prisoners. He was familiar with their graphic stories and the restoration and healing needed for the surviving prisoners afterward. We then quickly changed the subject and enjoyed the rest of our short visit together before he left to meet up with his family.

A Tool for the Gospel

Why am I bringing up the morbid subject of dungeons? I want you to know how people can be enslaved in a "spiritual dungeon" and must be set free, just like the vivid story Raymond shared about the WWII prisoners. We are here to set the captives free through the Word of God. The good news is that God is faithful.

Imagine if we could see with God's eyes in the spirit realm. We would probably see many people walking around with an invisible steel band around their foreheads, a chain around their necks, or even shackles on their feet. It's what we drag around with us as we go about our daily lives and what consistently nags us in our subconscious.

People can be enslaved in a "spiritual dungeon" and must be set free.

Enslavement means the state of being enslaved, slavery, bondage, servitude. Money and material possessions have attached demands on us for protection and maintenance. Thus, the things we own could soon own us.

Remember, a financial bondage is a yoke that prevents us from experiencing total freedom in our finances. God's Word has the answer to solve this problem and any other bondage we may face.

Counting the Cost

As of this writing, I have had the privilege of living in three different states. Every time my husband and I relocated, I had the opportunity to declutter my house and remove unused items. Of course, the other motive was so we would have fewer things to move. I regularly practice cleaning out the clutter in my home.

Before purchasing anything, I do my best to evaluate whether the item is necessary and what the cost of maintenance would be on it. I ask myself, "Can I afford this?" Not just in terms of the initial purchase price but also in terms of the time and money required to maintain the item afterward. Luke 14:28 says to count the cost before we begin to build something. "For which of you, intending to build a tower, does not sit down first and count the cost, whether he has enough to finish it." I believe this verse primarily refers to ensuring we have enough faith and resources to finish the project once it is started.

However, as you may know, some projects still need service even after they are built, and that is what I am referencing here. You may want to ask yourself, "How much of my time, physical maintenance, and money will this item cost me after I buy it?" "Do I need to purchase ongoing insurance on it?" "Are the benefits worth the initial and hidden costs of this asset over its lifetime?" After seeking God's wisdom and researching diligently, a final decision can be made confidently.

The Things We Own Could Soon Own Us

How do we become a slave to the things we own? The answer is simple. It's a heart issue. Financial freedom begins in your heart, not your bank account.

On a beautiful autumn day, with the sun glistening through the trees and the cool breeze blowing lightly on my body, I enjoy hiking on the mountain trails or even walking around my neighborhood. On my journey, I go places and see new things. There is a sensation of experiencing some sort of freedom.

When rain or snow interferes with my outdoor activities, I prefer exercising indoors at a local gym and using their various weight machines. There is heat in the winter and air conditioning in the summer. However, indoor activities do not provide the beautiful scenery or the sensation of freedom that outdoor activities offer.

I exercise because I like the benefits of it—whether

outdoors or indoors. I focus on the results or goal, not necessarily the means to achieve it. I am not a slave to the exercise machines. The gym membership, the weight bench at home, or my hiking boots are suitable investments, and they do not own me. I am not enslaved to them. I don't need them to impress other people. They are merely tools to help me accomplish my exercise goals.

The resources and money my husband and I sow into other faith-filled ministries that invest in advancing the Kingdom of God have eternal benefits. That money is a tool, and it does not own us. We have control over our resources and use them to bless others.

The Love of Money

A classic example of the enslavement bondage that comes to my mind is the image of a treadmill. You are walking on a machine and expending a lot of energy, but you're not going anywhere. Why are you accumulating wealth, gadgets, resources, and money? What's your main motive or goal? Is it to spend it all on yourself? Or are you trying to impress others with a status above your present financial resources?

I like the verse, 1 Timothy 6:9-10, in the J.B. Phillips New Testament Translation:

For men who set their hearts on being wealthy expose themselves to temptation. They fall into one of the world's oldest traps and lay themselves open to all sorts of silly and wicked desires, which are quite capable of utterly ruining and destroying their souls. For loving money leads to all kinds of evil, and some men in the struggle to be rich have lost their faith and caused themselves untold agonies of mind.

This verse says they set their hearts on wealth and silly and wicked desires instead of on God. They loved money instead of God. That is a good verse for understanding what enslaves us and what keeps our money from working for us.

Loving money or serving money more than God is an illusion we cannot afford. There's nothing but mental anguish that fills that road. Money, in and of itself, cannot buy us happiness. Chasing after money and material possessions will not give us the peace and freedom that we need in our souls. Money makes a very poor god.

In heaven, God uses gold to pave the streets. He has a different mindset of wealth than we do. We are made in His image, and we are His children. Thinking like our Father in Heaven with His standards and wisdom is the only way to enjoy true financial freedom. He is our wealthy Father in heaven.

Symptoms of Enslavement

How do you know if you are being enslaved? Here are some symptoms of being in the money and material possessions dungeon. See if any of these imprison you:

- Are you worried, fearful, and anxious about money?
- Are you constantly mismanaging your money?
- Are you making bad investments or overspending?
- Do you always say, "I can't afford it?"
- Are you driven to impulse buying?
- Are you stingy with how you spend your money?
- Do you look at others and long for what they have?
- Do you complain that you never have enough?
- Are you in bondage to looming debt and see no way out of it?

You can get out of the dungeon of enslavement

and be free. Financial freedom begins in your heart, not your bank account.

Acquiring Wisdom

Herein lies our hope - Proverbs 4:7-9 talks about a key to our freedom.

Wisdom is the principal thing; Therefore, get wisdom. And in all your getting, get understanding. Exalt her, and she will promote you; She will bring you honor when you embrace her. She will place on your head an ornament of grace; A crown of glory she will deliver to you. (Proverbs 4:7-9)

Wisdom is the principal thing—the main thing—the central focus. Where do we get wisdom? It is readily available in great abundance in the Word of God.

God's wisdom for handling money is so far beyond what any billionaire could offer as advice. We should be encouraged to turn our eyes away from Wall Street and onto what God's Word says about our wealth and finances.

Wisdom for how to get free and stay free truly starts in our hearts and minds. My favorite verse in the Bible is 3 John 2, which says, "Beloved, I pray that you may prosper in all things and be in health, just as your soul prospers." Our soul needs to prosper to bring wealth to our lives. Reading and meditating on verses in the Bible is the process of renewing the mind.

The Power to Change

The solution is simple, although it may take work at first. The Bible on our bookshelf, coffee table, or smartphone contains the key to our freedom. That powerful book is alive with God's wisdom to help us escape that enslavement bondage.

It's activating God's mind and living inside us daily that helps us make every purchase, plan, decision, and commitment based on biblical truth.

One wintery day, I was dressed in my heavy winter coat as I was volunteering outside as a greeter at the door of a ministry's building. A divine appointment with a young lady happily greeting at the door next to me awaited me. We began to engage in a fruitful conversation. She shared with me how, when she was growing up, her family used to read the Bible together, and her mother encouraged her to read it for herself daily. She knew the importance of the living Word of God and how it shaped and changed her life for the better. She had a personal relationship with Jesus in her heart at a very early age.

My story was a little different. When I was a little

girl growing up in New England, I also had Jesus, the living Word of God, but He was inside a giant family Bible sitting on top of the bookcase in my bedroom. At that time, I thought only the clergy could understand and interpret the Bible, so I never even attempted to read it.

Because I believed a lie growing up, I didn't know Jesus personally in my heart, even though the living Word of God existed in a huge Bible sitting on the bookcase in my bedroom. I knew about God, rosary prayers, and the apostle's creed, but it was more like a mental assent rather than a heartfelt revelation. Mental assent is when someone agrees with the Bible or God intellectually but doesn't have faith in God or the Bible for themselves.

The wisdom and power contained in the Word of God is what sets us free.

It was not until my early thirties that I accepted Jesus into my heart as my Savior and Lord. Suddenly, my life began to change. Thank God for His saving grace.

The wisdom and power contained in the Word of God is what sets us free. That's the key. The ability to get wealth doesn't come from the outside; it comes from inside our hearts, where Jesus lives.

Being a Partner with God

The Lord gives us money with a mission and prosperity with a purpose. He blesses us so that we can be a blessing to others.

Imagine what your life would be like if you could personally, one day, serve nourishing meals to 50 orphans in Africa and, at the same time, pay for a widow to buy a newer vehicle to improve her commute to work while also providing gasoline for an evangelist to start up generators in a large crusade to preach the gospel to the locals in Mexico. How could you do all this as just one person? You are not omnipresent. However, you could use your discretionary income and partner with God through other ministries to accomplish great things like these and so much more while never leaving your house.

In Deuteronomy 8:18, we read a well-known verse, "And you shall remember the LORD your God, for it is He who gives you power to get wealth, that He may establish His covenant which He swore to your fathers, as it is this day." When we are born again and become part of God's family, we enter an eternal relationship with the God of the universe, who has vast and intricate purposes for bringing

His covenant blessings to every man, woman, and child. Let God's heart of love be the heartbeat of your life, and let's see what God will do through you.

Praise the Lord for continuing this faith journey with us in financial freedom through the Word of God. I pray you have already defeated the previous giants that have come to steal your wealth and peace of mind. Stay the course. Don't quit! We are moving on to win over the "envy trap" giant next.

Through faith and patience, we will inherit the promises. "Do not become sluggish but imitate those who through faith and patience inherit the promises." (Hebrews 6:12)

God's Thoughts for Your Journey

Here are some powerful kingdom thoughts to meditate on and let them sink deep into your heart. They have the power to bring victory into your life and finances.

"Fear of the LORD is the foundation of true wisdom. All who obey his commandments will grow in wisdom." (Psalm 111:10 NLT)

"Then the trees of the field shall yield their fruit, and the earth shall yield her increase. They shall be safe in their land, and they shall know that I am the LORD, when I have broken the bands of their yoke and delivered them from the hand of those who enslaved them." (Ezekiel 34:27)

"So Jesus said to those Jews who had believed in Him, If you abide in My word [hold fast to My teachings and live in accordance with them], you are truly My disciples." (John 8:31 AMPC)

Chapter 7

The Envy Trap

It was a beautiful autumn morning in New England with a variety of colorful leaves on the trees. I enjoyed my drive into the office and was surprised when the phone rang as I entered the doorway. "Who could be calling me so early in the morning?" I thought. When I picked up the receiver, I recognized the soft voice at the other end of the phone, and it brought a smile to my face. It was Lisa, my young single mom client. Over the past year, I had been mentoring her in the ways of the Lord and finances. She was very hungry and open to learning more about being a good steward of her finances, growing in the Lord, and being a godly woman and a wife in the future. I know that seems like a tall order; however, we serve a big God, and nothing is impossible with God.

As Lisa described her situation, I immediately

understood the problem. Remember, we are on this journey toward financial freedom together. Along the way, we will encounter ugly giants such as insecurity, fear, anxiety, ungratefulness, enslavement, envy, bitterness, and disillusionment that loom in our hearts. These enemies have tormented us long enough, but no more! We are pressing on to learn the truth and apply it to our situations, using the spiritual weapons found in the Word of God and understanding how to live a prosperous life by faith.

We must know our enemy before we can defeat him. Be aware when the green-eyed monster of envy reveals its ugly head. Envy has at its core a social comparison in which one lacks something desirable that the other person has. Another way of describing envy is the painful feeling of wanting what someone else has, like attributes or possessions. Envy means to feel uneasiness, mortification, or discontent at the sight of superior excellence, reputation, or happiness enjoyed by another.

From a financial point of view, some of my potential clients often exhibited dissatisfaction with their current financial situation. They were trying to solve their problems by making irrational purchases in a fruitless attempt to compensate for their perceived lack. Spending money frivolously to fill a perceived void on the inside of their hearts doesn't work. We cannot solve a spiritual problem by using natural means. We need to go to the spiritual root in our hearts, which may take some time, effort, and motivation, but it is worth the journey.

You can probably imagine how quickly this envy monster can steal, kill, and destroy our prosperity and much of our earning potential. When our minds are cluttered, we are not open to the creative ideas and witty inventions the Lord has for us. Trying to get rid of the painful feeling of envy in our own limited strength and with our own resources becomes the focus of our mind. It darkens our unguarded hearts and blocks God's ideas for managing our financial affairs.

If you feel frustrated with your finances and are not as free as you'd like to be, there's probably a yoke preventing you from reaching your full potential. In this case, envy was Lisa's problem. Once her enemy was exposed, she was ready to defeat it.

How did she break free from the financial bondage of envy? We put together a spiritual plan of action to defeat it. Since envy results in comparison and prevents us from being content with what God has already given us to enjoy, the antidote is:

- Be willing to face our giant.
- Repent and turn to the Lord.
- Be thankful for what God has already provided for us.
- Enjoy our current blessings.

- Get God's vision about the good plan He has for us.

Habakkuk 2:2-3 says to write the vision, "Then the LORD answered me and said: "Write the vision and make it plain on tablets, that he may run who reads it. For the vision is yet for an appointed time; But at the end, it will speak, and it will not lie. though it tarries, wait for it; because it will surely come, it will not tarry."

When we seek God for a personal vision, our focus is redirected toward what God has for us and not toward what He has done in other people's lives by comparison. This practice can bring inner peace and anticipation of good things to come in our own lives when we see our vision from the heart of God written down. It is personal and intimate. Knowing God's plans for us ignites faith in our hearts and brings excitement for a brighter future.

The enemy of envy cannot exist in the presence of strong faith.

Once our giant is defeated and we choose to trust God, there is no longer a dependence upon our money to fill the void in our hearts. Impulse buying and frivolous spending will cease. Now, our financial decisions can be led by the Holy Spirit instead of trying to figure out how to meet our needs independently from God.

The enemy of envy cannot exist in the presence of strong faith. Just like Lisa was able to defeat her bondage, you can too.

Cain and Able

Let's look at a classic story in the Word of God that illustrates the "envy trap" and where sin could lead to destruction if it is not repented of. God takes this subject very seriously. Envy stirred up the first murder recorded in the Bible over the sensitive subject of an offering.

In the book of Genesis, Cain and Abel are introduced.

Now Adam knew Eve his wife, and she conceived and bore Cain, and said, "I have acquired a man from the LORD." Then she bore again, this time his brother Abel. Now Abel was a keeper of sheep, but Cain was a tiller of the ground. And in the process of time, it came to pass that Cain brought an offering of the fruit of the ground to the LORD. Abel also brought of the firstborn of his flock and of their fat. And the LORD respected Abel and his offering, but He did not respect Cain and his offering. And Cain was very angry, and his countenance fell. (Genesis 4:1-5)

Did you know that God does not accept every offering given to Him? Just because God is love and He loves mankind does not mean He has to receive every offering presented to Him. God recognized Abel's offering, but He did not accept Cain's.

By faith Abel offered to God a more excellent sacrifice than Cain, through which he obtained witness that he was righteous, God testifying of his gifts; and through it he being dead still speaks. By faith Enoch was taken away so that he did not see death, "and was not found, because God had taken him"; for before he was taken he had this testimony, that he pleased God. (Hebrews 11:4-5)

How do we please God? It is by faith in our hearts. What is inside our hearts is what will determine whether our offering is acceptable and pleasing to God or not. "But without faith it is impossible to please Him, for he who comes to God must believe that He is, and that He is a rewarder of those who diligently seek Him." (Hebrews 11:6).

Offerings are God's idea, and they matter to Him. From studying the offerings given by Cain and Able, it's important to realize that the Lord does not receive all offerings even though they are given to Him. God is looking at our hearts. Cain just brought an offering to the Lord in the process of time, in other words, when he felt like it. Abel's offering was timely, and he brought his best and his first. Abel had love, respect, and faith in his heart toward God when he brought his offering. Cain was just going through the ritual motions of giving. He did not give his first or his best.

Offerings are God's idea, and they matter to Him.

The Size of the Offering

Those who love God extravagantly give much to God. The chief expression of love is giving. John 3:16 is the most significant expression of love—God gave His only Son to die on the cross for our sins and redeem us to Himself. However, God doesn't look at who gave the largest dollar amount. That would mean only those with the greatest amount of money or goods could please God. That is not true. God looks at the heart.

I like the story of the widow with the two mites. Jesus said she put in more than everyone else. How can that be?

And He looked up and saw the rich putting their gifts into the treasury, and He saw also

*a certain poor widow putting in two mites.
So He said, "Truly I say to you that this poor
widow has put in more than all; for all these
out of their abundance have put in offerings
for God, but she out of her poverty put in all
the livelihood that she had. (Luke 21:1-4)*

God doesn't look at the dollar amount. He looks at
the percentage and the heart. The precious widow
gave 100%. She gave all that she had. That's the
only way she could have outgiven everybody else
giving into the treasury. God looks at the heart
and the percentage. It doesn't matter how big the
gifts might be. It is not about the amount or how
expensive the gift might be. God looks at the heart.

Freewill Offering

God Himself testified about Abel's offering. We
can see in Hebrews 11:4 that He took the time to
mention it. God did not testify about Cain's offering,
as there was little to say. What made Abel's offering
better than Cain's? What made his offering excellent
and acceptable? The Bible tells us it was Abel's faith.
He wanted to express his love toward the Father.

Cain brought his gift at the end of the day. It was
a ritual gift going through the motions, giving God
his leftovers. Abel had reverence and awe of God,
and he showed his love by giving God his first and

best offering. (See Gen 4:3). Abel's heart was filled with faith, and it showed up in his offering that pleased God. Imagine this: Abel's act of faith is still being discussed today.

There is a key spiritual principle here. Remember, financial freedom begins in your heart, not your bank account.

Cain was envious of Abel because his brother got God's attention with his gift, and he didn't. Have you ever entertained these thoughts put in your mind by the enemy as bait?

- Why don't I receive the attention of others that I long for?
- Why don't they notice me?
- What's wrong with me?
- Why do other people get all the attention and promotions from the boss, and I feel overlooked?
- Why can't I have what they have?

Comparing ourselves with others is dangerous and will never satisfy us. We can't have what someone else has unless we are willing to do what they did to get it. Although, some of us will never have the anointing to be a marathon runner if the muscles in our bodies are designed for sprinting. We often see the incredible outward benefits bestowed on others around us; however, we cannot see the inner workings of their heart of faith. That's God's job. Everyone's journey in this life is unique.

Discovering our individual calling, focusing on developing it, and trusting God in the process is best. God has a unique plan designed for each of us, and it is good. "For I know the plans I have for you," declares the LORD, "plans to prosper you and not to harm you, plans to give you hope and a future." (Jeremiah 29:11 NIV)

Envy Summary

In the Bible story, Cain directed his anger at Abel, a more tangible and visible target for his fury, and murdered him. Abel loved God. He gave with the right heart attitude.

Envy results from comparison. Cain compared himself to Abel and became envious of his brother. His envy resulted in murder.

Envy also prevents us from being content with what God has already given us to enjoy. Our powerful counterattack to envy would be contentment. 1 Timothy 6:6 says, "But godliness with contentment is great gain."

Comparison will try to rise its ugly head in our thought life. The lies bombarding our minds must be cast down quickly and lined up with the Word of

God. "We destroy every proud obstacle that keeps people from knowing God. We capture their rebellious thoughts and teach them to obey Christ." (2 Corinthians 10:5-6 NLT) It's too easy to compare ourselves with others rather than be content with what we presently have.

It can be challenging to keep your eyes focused on God and His plan for your life. After all, when you stand before God one day in heaven, He is not going to ask you about your neighbor. He is going to ask you if you did what He wanted you to do with the life and talents He gave you.

I know I want to stand in the presence of God and hear Him say, "Well done, good servant; because you were faithful in very little, have authority over ten cities." (Luke 19:17). How about you? What do you want to hear?

Be sure to guard your heart against this green-eyed monster of envy as you continue this financial freedom journey through the Word of God with us. Stand firm on the Scriptures, and do not let the enemy steal your stuff, your peace, or your grateful heart.

We are getting stronger and are ready to move

forward and defeat another financial bondage with the Word of God. This giant is named bitterness!

God's Thoughts for Your Journey

Here are some powerful kingdom thoughts to meditate on and let them sink deep into your heart. They have the power to bring prosperity into your life and finances.

"The generous soul will be made rich, And he who waters will also be watered himself." (Proverbs 11:25)

"All praise to God, the Father of our Lord Jesus Christ. God is our merciful Father and the source of all comfort. He comforts us in all our troubles so that we can comfort others. When they are troubled, we will be able to give them the same comfort God has given us." (2 Corinthians 1:3-4)

"Now faith is the assurance (the confirmation, the title deed) of the things [we] hope for, being the proof of things [we] do not see and the conviction of their reality [faith perceiving as real fact what is not revealed to the senses]." (Hebrews 11:1 AMPC)

Chapter 8

Bitterness Made Sweet

It was a beautiful sunny day outside, and my husband and I were relaxing on the deck when I heard him say, "Do you want to eat some ice cream?" As I listened to those inviting words, my mouth began to water, and I started imagining my favorite flavor of ice cream. Of course, I said, "Yes!" Growing up in New England, I have many fond memories of eating ice cream. This treat reminds me of something sweet, creamy, and delicious, and it satisfies my palate better than any other dessert. I find I enjoy eating something sweet over something bitter.

While I was enjoying my ice cream and how sweet it tasted, the Holy Spirit reminded me of Psalm 119:103, of how His words are sweet and desirable, too. "How sweet are Your words to my taste, Sweeter than honey to my mouth!" (Psalm 119:103) The Word of God may not be the same as ice cream; however, both are sweet and, for me, much preferred over anything bitter, wouldn't you agree?

As we all know and may agree, life is not always as sweet as ice cream. Unfair situations and offenses will come our way, and if we allow the enemy to, he will use those opportunities to ignite anger and resentment in our emotions. Bitterness can affect our financial goals and, if left unchecked, as I learned, may become a financial bondage that will hinder our hearts from prospering in the Lord and in our finances.

Turn On the Light

I remember a time when I was young in my knowledge of the Lord and fell victim to the bondage of bitterness. In my heart, I knew something was wrong, but at the time, I did not have enough spiritual wisdom to discern what the problem was. You could say I was blinded by it. In those moments, God placed mature Christian people in my path to help me pray and eliminate the root bitterness that was hiding in my heart.

The lesson I learned was that focusing on hurtful situations, nursing grudges filled with resentment, and allowing hostility to stay in my heart was a breeding ground for the enemy of bitterness. Did you notice I said the word "learned?" I had to learn what harboring bitterness meant. It is clearer to me now; however, looking back on my life, I simply couldn't see it. Bitterness blinded my eyes and my heart. I'm so grateful for God's mercy and grace toward me during the time of learning His Words and how to apply His truth to my life.

When we hang around others filled with bitterness, we can quickly adopt bitterness as a normal response to life's circumstances. I began to see the value of surrounding myself with people who made wise and positive choices. Their characters began to influence mine. "Do not be deceived: "Evil company corrupts good habits." (1 Corinthians 15:33). As I learned how to be more positive and joyful, my life began to change for the better, and that led to seeing more favorable results.

When the light is turned on in a dark room, we can see the obstacles in our way. Spiritual darkness is no different; it requires the light to be turned on to recognize what is harmful and displeasing to God. If we allow negative thoughts to crowd out our positive thoughts, we might be swallowed up by bitterness or a sense of injustice. Once our eyes are opened to this insidious bondage, it can be immediately destroyed through repentance and forgiveness.

My desire is to see us all free from bitterness. I know it is too easy to hold on to this destructive habit of harboring bitterness, but I encourage you to let go of the hurt. Cast all your cares on the Lord because He cares for you. "Casting the whole of your care [all your anxieties, all your worries, all your concerns, once and for all] on Him, for He cares for you affectionately and cares about you watchfully." (1 Peter 5:7 AMPC)

God wants us to be free like He is - to think like Him, to act like Him, to speak like Him, and to give like Him. I can assure you that bitterness has no place in God. He is love. "He who does not love does not know God, for God is love." (1 John 4:8).

A Biblical Perspective of Victory

If anyone had cause to be bitter, it was Joseph in the Bible. His brothers despised him because of his dreams, brutally sold him into slavery, and then lied to their father that a wild animal had killed him. Joseph spent time in prison on false charges of rape and was left there for two years longer because Pharaoh's forgetful chief butler forgot his promise to help get Joseph out of prison. Despite all this, here's how Joseph reconciled with his brothers in Genesis 45:4-15.

And Joseph said to his brothers, "Please come near to me." So they came near. Then he said: "I am Joseph, your brother, whom you sold into Egypt. But now, do not therefore be grieved or angry with yourselves because you sold me here, for God sent me before you to preserve life. For these two years, the famine has been in the land, and there are still five years in which there will be neither plowing nor harvesting. And God sent me before you to preserve a posterity for you in the earth and to save your lives by a great deliverance. So now it was not you who sent me here, but God; and He has made me a father to Pharaoh, and lord of all his house, and a ruler throughout all the land of Egypt.

"Hurry and go up to my father, and say to him, 'Thus says your son Joseph: "God has made me lord of all Egypt; come down to me, do not tarry. You shall dwell in the land of Goshen, and you shall be near to me, you and your children, your children's children, your flocks and your herds, and all that you have. There I will provide for you, lest you and your household, and all that you have come to poverty, for there are still five years of famine."'

"And behold, your eyes and the eyes of my brother Benjamin see that it is my mouth that speaks to you. So you shall tell my father of all my glory in Egypt, and of all that you have seen; and you shall hurry and bring my father down here."

*Then he fell on his brother Benjamin's neck
and wept, and Benjamin wept on his neck.
Moreover, he kissed all his brothers and wept
over them, and after that, his brothers talked
with him. (Genesis 45:4-15)*

When Joseph asked his brothers to come near to
him, he wasn't fearful they would harm him again.
He followed God's example and showed them unconditional love. Then Joseph released them from any
grief or guilt for their past actions of selling him
into slavery and didn't condemn them for their
prior rejection and violent behavior toward him.
Nor did Joseph blame his brothers for the pain he
experienced in his past. Joseph saw God's plan working "behind the scenes" in his life for the benefit
of others, especially his family and was willing to
share it with them.

Joseph was ready to have his brothers come live
on the land near him, and he would provide for all
of them. He was excited about reconciling with his
entire family, kissing and hugging them, and loving
on them forever. What a beautiful picture this is of
the reconciliation we have through our Lord and
Savior, Jesus Christ.

The Old Testament character of Joseph is a type
and shadow of Jesus who loves us, forgives our sins,
restores us, provides for us, wants us to live close to

Him as family members, and enjoys being together with us in His kingdom forever.

The Choices We Make

Joseph chose not to be bitter toward his brothers. He guarded his heart and focused on God's plan for his life by not comparing himself to his brothers nor mourning over all the injustices done to him in the past. He continued to prosper while in prison and celebrated God's plan for his life.

What would have happened if Joseph embraced bitterness? If he chose to hold on to bitterness and exhibit anger and disappointment at being mistreated unfairly, his life could have turned out very differently. We can only speculate the answer to that question based on God's Word. The Word warns us against the dangers of bitterness. Proverbs 18:19 says, "A brother offended is harder to win than a strong city, And contentions are like the bars of a castle."

The way to get rid of the bondage of bitterness is through repentance and forgiveness.

If we choose to allow bitterness a place in our

hearts, it can poison our journey toward wealth in God. We can erect invisible walls to hide behind and isolate ourselves from other people. This is a false sense of protection, and it can contaminate our entire generational line if left unresolved. Bitter people tend to pass bitterness on from one generation to the next. It must be uprooted. The way to get rid of the bondage of bitterness is through repentance and forgiveness.

Joseph made the right choice, refusing to be bitter and choosing forgiveness. You can make the right choice, as well.

How to Overcome the Invisible Walls of Isolation

Over the years, I have had my share of relationship hurts, betrayals, and rejections. How about you? Bitterness crept into my heart more than once, and I had to evict it. The Word of God tells us to get rid of it. "Get rid of all bitterness, rage, anger, harsh words, and slander, as well as all types of evil behavior. Instead, be kind to each other, tenderhearted, forgiving one another, just as God through Christ has forgiven you." (Ephesians 4:31-32 NLT)

I've found that the best way to overcome bitterness is to do it the Lord's way. He says to replace bitterness with love, kindness, and forgiveness.

Although that sounds simple and may be challenging to do, it is freeing at the same time. The Word of God says, "For with God nothing will be impossible." (Luke 1:37)

Living free of bitterness requires repentance. According to Strong's concordance, the Greek word for "repent" is Metanoeo (G3340), which means "To change one's mind, to change one's mind for better, heartily to amend with abhorrence of one's past sins."

The decision to turn away from sin allows us to experience God's love. He will not force us to change our minds—He gave us free will to choose for ourselves.

There are many negative things listed in Ephesians 4:31—bitterness, wrath, anger, clamor, and malice—that we are to put away. This does not mean that we are to spend endless nights trying to rid ourselves of bitterness. That's fruitless self-effort. The good news is that God has equipped us with the power and ability to do so in the following verse. We have what it takes to defeat the giant of bitterness that tries to invade our hearts.

In Ephesians 4:32, God instructs us what to put on kindness, tenderheartedness, and forgiveness. God wants us to turn away from focusing on the negative and to "put on" kindness, tenderheartedness, and forgiveness. He knows we cannot focus on two things at the same time. When we give God's Word first place in our hearts, it opens the door for us to receive more of God's goodness and sets us free from bitterness.

Receiving our personal forgiveness from God empowers us to forgive others.

It's refreshing to know that the Lord, in His love and grace, has already delivered us from all sin, including bitterness. When we accept Jesus as our Lord and Savior and follow up with corresponding action, we are set free from sin and death.

Speaking what you believe out loud is the corresponding action to what you believe in your heart. "That if you confess with your mouth the Lord Jesus and believe in your heart that God has raised Him from the dead, you will be saved. For with the heart one believes unto righteousness, and with the mouth confession is made unto salvation." (Romans 10:9-10)

Receiving our personal forgiveness from God empowers us to forgive others. After all, we can't give away what we don't have. Forgiveness is a key we can use against the enemy attacking our hearts.

Overturning Thoughts of Bitterness

Has your mind ever been bombarded with terrible thoughts about someone? I know mine has. I remember a time when my mind was under serious attack. On this perfectly beautiful day, as I was doing chores around my house, I kept hearing these negative lies attacking my mind about my husband. Maybe you've heard similar accusations like, "He never does what you ask him to do for you." "He is irresponsible and never completes anything." "He doesn't care about God or you." Of course, all these statements are outright lies! The enemy stages these lies as bait to see if we would believe them.

What if I meditated on these lies during the day and agreed with them? They would have painted an evil picture on the inside of my mind about my husband and created a breeding ground for darkness. The accusations were meant to create division in our marriage and breed anger and bitterness in my heart toward him. How could I possibly "see" my husband as the wonderful, loving, godly man that he is if I am believing the crafty lies of the enemy about him?

Here is the revelation I received that day. I had a

choice to make. Whose report was I going to believe? Isaiah 53:1 says it clearly, "Who has believed our report? And to whom has the arm of the LORD been revealed?" To see the arm of the Lord revealed in my life, I needed to agree with God. The arm of the Lord symbolizes spiritual strength or power. And that is what I did - I chose to believe the report of the Lord about my husband and considered him to be a Psalm 112 righteous man. As I stood confidently in my position of faith, I received God's strength to overcome the enemy's lies.

When my husband came home that day, he had no idea of all the accusations I could have dumped on him. Instead, I responded to him with kindness and love because I chose not to believe any of the false accusations I heard in my mind. And what kind of response do you think I received in return from my husband? He reciprocated in kindness and love just like the wonderful, loving, godly man he is. Praise the Lord! Doing things God's way and agreeing with His Word brings rewards.

If I allowed bitterness to fester in my heart, then I would have agreed with the enemy and fallen victim to confusion, and forfeited my reward. "For where envying and strife is, there is confusion and every evil work." (James 3:16 KJV). Remember, financial freedom begins in your heart, not your bank account.

How did this affect our finances? My husband

and I received favor from God and were blessed with many opportunities to meet new people. This time, our reward did not manifest itself in mere dollars and cents. It came through long-lasting divine appointments and relationships with others that resulted in our needs being abundantly supplied.

God did exceedingly abundantly above all that I could ask or even think. "Now to Him who is able to do exceedingly abundantly above all that we ask or think, according to the power that works in us, to Him be glory in the church by Christ Jesus to all generations, forever and ever. Amen." (Ephesians 3:20-21)

Forgiveness

Life can be challenging and complicated at times. But God's goodness remains throughout every season, and He is always faithful. He paid an ultimate price to give us everlasting life, hope, peace, and a bright future. Why would anyone want to hold on to a man-made prison of bitterness when they can receive such wonderful freedom and joy from God?

For myself, forgiving other people, blessing them, and basking in God's love for me has helped me overcome the enemy of bitterness when it tries to attack my heart. Healing and freedom are available to us as we make the right choices. God loves us, and He will surely help us.

And what does all this have to do with finances? Plenty! Because if our hearts are free, we are no longer in bondage. We are free to give. We are free to receive. We are free to manage all the goodness that we receive. And finally, we are free to love God, partner with Him, and help others by going beyond ourselves and expanding God's Kingdom on this earth.

Thank you for continuing with us on this powerful journey of Financial Freedom Through the Word of God. There is a reward waiting for us as we diligently seek the Lord. "But without faith it is impossible to please Him, for he who comes to God must believe that He is, and that He is a rewarder of those who diligently seek Him." (Hebrews 11:6).

In the next chapter, we have one more bondage to uncover before we solve the financial ownership question—who owns what? I encourage you to press onward. You can do it!

God's Thoughts for Your Journey

Here are some powerful kingdom thoughts to meditate on and let them sink deep into your heart. They have the power to bring victory into your life and finances.

"Then Peter came to Him and said, 'Lord, how often shall my brother sin against me, and I forgive him? Up to seven times?' Jesus said to him, 'I do not say to you, up to seven times, but up to seventy times seven.'" (Matthew 18:21-22)

"And be kind to one another, tenderhearted, forgiving one another, even as God in Christ forgave you." (Ephesians 4:32)

"Pursue peace with all people, and holiness, without which no one will see the Lord: looking carefully lest anyone fall short of the grace of God; lest any root of bitterness springing up cause trouble, and by this many become defiled." (Hebrews 12:14-15)

Chapter 9

Disillusionment Uncovered

Caleb blurted loudly as he sat facing my desk, leaning forward with a serious look on his face, waiting for my response to his question, "What am I going to do now?" Caleb was a single young man with a promising career. He just found out his fiancée was not being honest with him when she abruptly broke off their engagement. Caleb was extremely disappointed due to his efforts in diligently planning his entire financial future with her in mind.

Disappointments are a part of life. How we handle them determines our success and ability to move forward. I reassured Caleb that we would make all the necessary financial adjustments to his accounts without a problem.

However, I could understand that his emotions

were tied to his financial decisions and goals. Have you ever put your heart into an investment and had your hopes dashed? Perhaps you had great expectations for a raise or promotion only to find out you didn't qualify or weren't even considered for it?

Disillusionment is the last financial bondage I'm going to mention for now. On our journey to financial freedom, we may encounter other bondages or yokes that prevent us from experiencing total freedom in our hearts and finances. I believe the same tools given throughout this journey for dealing with the previous bondages can be applied to defeat any others that try to raise their ugly heads in the future.

Deceptive Appearance

Disillusionment is a separation or a parting from something. It shows a deceptive appearance or a false show, by which a person may be deceived or his expectations disappointed. In the area of finances, disillusionment can result when we try to use money to make us happy and bring us fulfillment in our lives. Material things only result in temporary pleasure, and when the novelty wears off, they often leave us feeling empty inside. Only God and His love can satisfy all our needs and innermost desires.

"Delight yourself also in the LORD, and He shall give you the desires of your heart." (Psalm 37:4).

"Do you mean, if I just delight myself in the Lord, He will automatically give me everything I want?" Caleb asked sarcastically. I responded, "That's a good question and an interesting way of putting it." Based on the tone of his voice, I responded gently, "When you delight yourself in the Lord, God places His desires in your heart."

Only God and His love can satisfy all our needs and innermost desires.

How do we delight ourselves in the Lord? Delight means to take great pleasure in or to give joy or satisfaction to. Here are two questions I gave Caleb to ponder:

- Are you excited to spend time in the presence of the Lord, listening to His voice and hearing His plans for your life?

  OR

- Do you prefer making your own plans based on your fleshly desires or what you see other people doing that looks good to you and then asking God to bless your ideas?

Caleb looked away from me and contemplated my questions intently for a long period of time in silence before he made the quality decision to seek God first and discover God's plan for his life. He could see how Psalm 37:4 could work in his life. The practice of delighting, meditating, and confessing the Word of God is what paints an inner image on the inside of us authored by God Himself.

"So shall My word be that goes forth from My mouth; It shall not return to Me void, But it shall accomplish what I please, And it shall prosper in the thing for which I sent it." (Isaiah 55:11). God is obligated to fulfill His Word.

After a lengthy conversation with Caleb in my office, he finally reached a peaceful place of understanding in his heart concerning the future direction of his accounts. Caleb was excited to begin his new financial journey God's way. Remember, financial freedom begins in your heart, not your bank account.

My Utmost for His Highest

When I was single, I used to read the classic devotional literature by Oswald Chambers called "My Utmost for His Highest."

Oswald Chambers was born in Scotland and spent much of his boyhood there. His ministry of teaching and preaching took him to the United States and Japan for a time. The last six years of his life were spent as a principal of the Bible Training College in London and as a chaplain to British Commonwealth troops in Egypt during World War l. After his death, the books which bear his name were compiled by his wife from her own verbatim shorthand notes of his talks.

Here is one of his teachings about disillusionment:

The Teaching of Disillusionment

Jesus did not commit Himself to them..., for He knew what was in man.

John 2:24-25

Disillusionment means having no more misconceptions, false impressions, and false judgments in life; it means being free from these deceptions. However, though no longer deceived, our experience of disillusionment may actually leave us cynical and overly critical in our judgment of others. But the disillusionment that comes from God brings us to the point where we see people as they really are, yet without any cynicism or any stinging and bitter criticism. Many of the things in life that inflict the greatest injury, grief, or pain stem from the fact that we suffer from illusions. We are not true to one another as facts, seeing each other as we really are; we are only true to our misconceived ideas of one another. According to our thinking, everything is either delightful and good or it is evil, malicious, and cowardly.

Refusing to be disillusioned is the cause of much of the suffering of human life. And this is how that suffering happens— if we love someone but do not love God, we demand total perfection and righteousness from that person, and when we do not get it, we become cruel and vindictive; yet we are demanding a human being something which he or she cannot possibly give. There is only one Being who can completely satisfy to the absolute depth of the hurting human heart, and that is the Lord Jesus Christ. Our Lord is so obviously uncompromising about every human relationship because He knows that every relationship that is not based on faithfulness to Himself will end in disaster. Our Lord trusted no one and never placed His faith in people, yet He was never suspicious or bitter. Our Lord's confidence in God, and in what God's grace could do for anyone, was so perfect that He never despaired, never giving up hope for any person. If our trust is placed in human beings, we will end up despairing of everyone.

My Honeymoon Experience

What a perfect description of disillusionment by Oswald Chambers. His devotional book was one of my favorite things to read first thing in the morning during my season of singleness. Just because I liked to get up at 5 am in the morning when I was single and read "My Utmost for His Highest" didn't mean my newly married husband would want to do the same thing, especially on our honeymoon.

I was surprised at my husband's response when I woke up early on the first morning after we married to read my favorite devotional, assuming he was going to join me. He did not look too favorably on my "religious routine." He preferred to take a walk on the beach and look at the dolphins swimming in the ocean of St. Pete Beach along the coast of Florida.

Of course, when I was young and immature, I thought I was the one who was right and my husband was the one who was wrong and not spiritual. We laugh at our past mistakes today. As I matured and reminisced on our honeymoon disagreement, I now understand that I was the one who was disillusioned. I had unreasonable expectations for my husband. He is the spiritual head and is responsible for leading us together as a married couple. Although we have our times of prayer and devotion together, we also have our separate private times of personal devotion with the Lord. God has a plan and purpose for each one of us, and finding that destiny is what truly fits and satisfies us at the core of our being.

Only God and His love can satisfy all our needs and innermost desires. "Delight yourself also in the LORD, and He shall give you the desires of your heart." (Psalm 37:4).

How to Remove Financial Bondages

Many financial bondages have been highlighted in the previous chapters for the purpose of revealing common obstacles in our hearts that could prevent us from experiencing financial freedom. How do we break free from these bondages, especially this disillusionment one?

First, we must recognize that we have them. If we ask God to reveal what is hindering us, He will show us. Also, trusted close friends can sometimes enlighten us about our blind spots or bondages. "In the same way that iron sharpens iron, a person sharpens the character of his friend." (Proverbs 27:17 VOICE)

Listen to what we say and the tone of voice we use to say it. Often, the words of our mouths reveal what is in our hearts. "A good man out of the good treasure of his heart brings forth good, and an evil man out of the evil treasure of his heart brings forth evil. For out of the abundance of the heart his mouth speaks." (Luke 6:45).

When the Lord reveals a bondage to us, it's best to decide we no longer want to wallow in it and that we want to be free from it. It is the quality decision we make to change our hearts and turn away from the revealed bondage that will propel us toward freedom.

> *If we confess our sins, He is faithful and just to forgive us our sins and to cleanse us from all unrighteousness. If we say that we have not sinned, we make Him a liar, and His word is not in us. My little children, these things I write to you, so that you may not sin. And if anyone sins, we have an Advocate with the Father, Jesus Christ the righteous. And He Himself is the propitiation for our sins, and not for ours only but also for the whole world. (1 John 1:9-2:2).*

Forgiveness in our hearts is a powerful force. Just as it can manifest healing in our bodies, it can also do miracles in our finances. How? Because financial freedom begins in your heart, not your bank account.

It is not enough to just turn away from something; we also need to turn our hearts toward something else. The best way to change our focus is to look on Jesus and the freedom we have available in Christ. Receiving God's grace—forgiveness of sins and His gift of righteousness in Christ Jesus is our new focus.

"For if by the one man's offense death reigned through the one, much more those who receive abundance of grace and of the gift of righteousness will reign in life through the One, Jesus Christ." (Romans 5:17).

Walk in the Spirit

How do we stay free of financial bondages? To remain free, we walk in the spirit. "I say then: Walk in the Spirit, and you shall not fulfill the lust of the flesh." (Galatians 5:16).

The simplest way to explain walking in the spirit is to follow what God's Word says.

The simplest way to explain walking in the spirit is to follow what God's Word says. When we read His Word, spend time in His presence, and pray, we can ask God to reveal Himself to us. When thoughts that are contrary to God's Word come into our minds, we must cast them down with the words of our mouth and replace them with what God's Word says about us. This is a lifelong learning process. The more we practice it, the better we'll get at it.

The opposite of walking in the spirit is walking in the flesh, which is referred to as being carnally minded. Being led by our five natural senses—sight, hearing, taste, smell, and touch—is being carnally minded and does not please God. "For to be carnally minded is death, but to be spiritually minded is life and peace. Because the carnal mind is enmity against God; for it is not subject to the law of God, nor indeed can be. So then, those who are in the flesh cannot please God." (Romans 8:6-8)

God wants us to follow His ways and plans for our lives and finances. "God is Spirit, and those who worship Him must worship in spirit and truth." (John 4:24)

Summary of Steps to Freedom

Although this may be an oversimplification of the steps to financial freedom that begin in our hearts, it can be used as a quick reference guide to help us along the way.

1. SEE the obstacles that are hindering us.
2. ADMIT they are blocking our freedom.

3. CHOOSE to change our mind and be free from them.
4. RECEIVE God's grace and forgiveness.
5. RENEW our mind to the truth in Scripture by focusing on Jesus.
6. WALK in the Spirit and not in the flesh.

And what does all this have to do with finances? Plenty! Because if our hearts are free, we are no longer in bondage. We are free to give. We are free to receive. We are free to manage all the goodness that we receive. And finally, we are free to love God, partner with Him, and help others by going beyond ourselves and expanding God's Kingdom on this earth.

We are continuing this journey and building something great in us that will last for all eternity. Thank you for joining us and for staying the course. Keep moving forward.

Let's continue together and answer the ownership question next. When our financial house is built on the solid foundation of the Word of God, it will not collapse during the storms of life. We are now introducing "the money part."

God's Thoughts for Your Journey

Here are some powerful kingdom thoughts to meditate on and let them sink deep into your heart. They have the power to bring prosperity into your life and finances.

"Write the vision And make it plain on tablets, That he may run who reads it. For the vision is yet for an appointed time; But at the end it will speak, and it will not lie. Though it tarries, wait for it; Because it will surely come, It will not tarry." (Habakkuk 2:2-3)

There is therefore now no condemnation to those who are in Christ Jesus, who do not walk according to the flesh, but according to the Spirit. For the law of the Spirit of life in Christ Jesus has made me free from the law of sin and death. For what the law could not do in that it was weak through the flesh, God did by sending His own Son in the likeness of sinful flesh, on account of sin: He condemned sin in the flesh, that the righteous requirement of the law might be fulfilled in us who do not walk according to the flesh but according to the Spirit. (Romans 8:1-4)

Love endures long and is patient and kind; love never is envious nor boils over with jealousy, is not boastful or vainglorious, does not display itself haughtily. It is not conceited (arrogant and inflated with pride); it is not rude (unmannerly) and does not act unbecomingly. Love (God's love in us) does not insist on its own rights or its own way, for it is not self-seeking; it is not touchy or fretful or resentful; it takes no account of the evil done to it [it pays no attention to a suffered wrong]. It does not rejoice at injustice and unrighteousness, but rejoices when right and truth prevail. Love bears up under anything and everything that comes, is ever ready to believe the best of every person, its hopes are fadeless under all circumstances, and it endures everything [without weakening]. Love never fails [never fades out or becomes obsolete or comes to an end]. (1 Corinthians 13:4-8a AMPC)

Chapter 10

The Ownership Question

The phone rang and it was the automotive company asking to speak with my husband. Although he was in his 20s, he still remembers the incident vividly. The company also preceded the phone call with a letter containing the same alarming news. After listening to what the people had to say on the phone from the credit department, my husband responded politely, "How can I be delinquent on my car payment? I made a few extra payments before they were due. I should be ahead of the schedule and not behind!" When he purchased a new truck, he took out a loan and assumed that because he had made extra payments ahead of time, he could skip one month and start again the following month.

He was in for a rude awakening. The loan's paperwork stipulated he must make monthly payments, regardless of how many payments he makes in advance. Somehow, he missed seeing that part in the fine print. The credit company also threatened to repossess the truck if he didn't make the next monthly payment.

How can the loan agency take such dramatic measures when he missed one month's payment and yet had made extra scheduled payments? The answer is simple. The credit company owns the vehicle until the loan is paid in full and the title is transferred to the buyer.

It didn't take my husband long to obtain wisdom on how to handle this situation in the future. He made the monthly payment. However, going forward, instead of making extra payments to the credit company in advance, he decided to make extra payments to his personal savings account. In the event he was ever short on funds in any given month to make his loan payment, he could then withdraw from his savings account. And in the meantime, he was earning interest on his personal bank account. My husband saw the benefits of ownership and, in the process of time, paid the loan off in full, earlier than the maturity date.

The wisdom of God in Proverbs 22:7 says, "The rich rules over the poor, And the borrower is servant to the lender." God wants us to be the lender and not the borrower and the head and not the tail. "And the LORD will make you the head and not the tail; you shall be above only, and not be beneath, if you heed the commandments of the LORD your God, which I command you today, and are careful to observe them." (Deuteronomy 28:13)

God wants us to be an owner like He is.

Ownership Privileges and Responsibilities

Many people want to know what the Bible says about owning things. They ask, "Do I own things, or does God own them? If God owns the cattle on a thousand hills, what do I own?" That's a good question.

The Biblical principle of ownership involves recognizing that all we have presently or all we will have in the future ultimately belongs to God. He has entrusted us with these resources and responsibilities to steward for His glory.

Let's find out what God owns. God gave us life. We didn't cause ourselves to exist. God created us in His image and likeness. Genesis 1:26 says, "Then God said, "Let Us make man in Our image, according to Our likeness; let them have dominion over the fish of the sea, over the birds of the air, and over the cattle, over all the earth and over every creeping thing that creeps on the earth."

God gave us special gifts and abilities when we were born. He has a plan and a purpose for us to fulfill in our lifetime while we are here on this earth. Romans 11:29 says God will not change His mind about what He has called us to do. "For the gifts and the calling of God are irrevocable." (Romans 11:29). Since God has called us and blessed us with gifts, that calling or plan is still there, whether we cooperate with it or not.

Will you cooperate with God's plan for your life and His way of doing things with your finances?

Created ~ Equipped ~ Called

What does it mean to be created by God, to be equipped with special gifts, and called to be His people? It's a sobering thought to believe we belong to a God Who created us and that we are not our own self-made person. In this world today, people want to do their own thing and have it their own way—just like the words in the song sung by Frank Sinatra say, "I did it, I did it My Way!" This attitude is appealing to our fleshly nature. However, in the Kingdom of God, things are the opposite.

I remember taking a field trip to the Old Sturbridge Village on a beautiful summer day when I lived in New England. This outdoor history museum celebrates the people who lived in rural New England in the formative first decades of our new nation – the United States of America. The Village provides an authentic, first-hand look at the often challenging and rapidly changing textures and rhythms of New England life in the transformative years—1790 to 1840. The Village uses its historic buildings and landscapes, expansive collections, and programs in agriculture, horticulture, households, and trades to produce innovative and engaging exhibitions, educational offerings, and public events.

I walked into one of the old buildings and saw the potter crafting his handiwork. He was mostly working with clay, fashioning pots, bowls, plates, and beautiful pottery vases by hand. Sometimes, he used a blueprint to create a unique vase for a specific purpose.

Did the special clay vase create itself? No. The potter created the artistic or functional objects from the clay, and so it is with God, our heavenly Father. He is likened to the Potter, and we, His children, are likened to the clay.

We are fashioned by our Creator and are not our own design. "...Who are you, a mere human being, to argue with God? Should the thing that was created say to the one who created it, "Why have you made me like this?" When a potter makes jars out of clay, doesn't he have a right to use the same lump of clay to make one jar for decoration and another to throw garbage into?" (Romans 9:20-21)

We Are Not Our Own

We are not our own. We belong to the Lord. I know some people may not like the idea of belonging to someone else. Our fleshly desire may want to be our own boss and determine our own destiny apart from God. However, the Scriptures clearly reveal who we really are.

> **We are not our own. We belong to the Lord.**

a. "Do you not know that you are the temple of God and that the Spirit of God dwells in you?" (1 Corinthians 3:16). God chose to live inside us. What an honor and a privilege that is to us.

b. "You were bought with a price..." (1 Corinthians 7:23). The price was the precious blood of Jesus.

c. "Know that the Lord, He is God; It is He who has made us, and not we ourselves; We are His people and the sheep of His pasture." (Psalm 100:3). We did not, nor could we create ourselves in the image of God.

d. "You are worthy, O Lord, To receive glory and honor and power; For You created all things, and by Your will they exist and were created." (Revelation 4:11). God created all things—everything—including us.

We will learn along this wonderful journey that God's faithful love endures forever, and He has great plans for us to partner with Him in advancing His Kingdom here on this earth.

Our Finances

So, if we are not our own, what makes us think our finances are our own? God owns everything. God owns our finances and us. Our financial journey is exciting because we have a loving heavenly Father who has our best interests in mind and has no limitations in His Kingdom.

a. "The earth is the LORD's, and all its fullness, The world and those who dwell therein." (Psalm 24:1).
b. "For every beast of the forest is Mine, And the cattle on a thousand hills." (Psalm 50:10).
c. "'The silver is Mine, and the gold is Mine,' says the LORD of Hosts." (Haggai 2:8).

Because God owns everything, including our finances and ourselves, it is important to develop a mindset of being a good steward of what He has given us. We possess things and have things in our possession, but God owns them.

Every gift of God comes with the responsibility to be a faithful steward of those resources. When I married my husband, his assets became mine too, the moment I said, "I do." Because I honor God and my husband, I choose to be a faithful steward of the resources bestowed to me through our marriage covenant. My husband and I prepare a budget and agree together on how our combined finances will be spent to accomplish God's purpose in our lives.

We do not even earn our income independently from God. The Word warns us against saying in our hearts, "My power and the might of my hand have gained me this wealth." (Deuteronomy 8:17). We are to give the praise and glory to God where it is due.

Every gift of God comes with the responsibility to be a faithful steward of those resources.

The Word continues saying, "And you shall remember the Lord your God, for it is He who gives you power to get wealth, that He may establish His covenant which He swore to your fathers, as it is this day." (Deuteronomy 8:18). We earn our wages; however, God enables

130

us to do so. Wealth comes to us by God's power, not by our own.

God wants us to partner with Him on this earth by using the resources He supplies to establish His covenant. What does "Establish His covenant mean?" God has extended to us a special invitation to join ourselves to Him in a personal relationship. When we do, the new covenant is between Almighty God and Jesus, so we can't mess it up. The covenant is filled with all of God's blessings. As with any relationship, it requires maintenance. Relationships need nurturing. (If you would like to receive Jesus as your Savior, please see the prayer at the end of this book.)

Let me go a step further: after we have established a personal relationship with Jesus and entered the covenant with God, He wants us to tell others about this covenant. Everyone can have forgiveness of their sins, be healed, set free, delivered, and blessed too. They can choose to have a personal relationship with their Creator.

Partnering with God and establishing His covenant on this earth requires love, time, and resources. We are God's hands and feet on this earth. He is looking to us to partner with Him and fulfill the great commission—to go into all the world and share the Gospel.

And He said to them, "Go into all the world

and preach the gospel to every creature. He who believes and is baptized will be saved; but he who does not believe will be condemned. And these signs will follow those who believe: In My name they will cast out demons; they will speak with new tongues; they will take up serpents; and if they drink anything deadly, it will by no means hurt them; they will lay hands on the sick, and they will recover." (Mark 16:15-18)

Joint Heirs

When we receive Jesus as our Savior and Lord and enter covenant with God, our position in life is now elevated to one of sonship. We are joint heirs with Christ. Therefore, we own everything God owns. And He has given us the responsibility of stewardship over all His awesome resources. "The Spirit Himself bears witness with our spirit that we are children of God, and if children, then heirs—heirs of God and joint heirs with Christ, if indeed we suffer with Him, that we may also be glorified together." (Romans 8:16-18)

An heir receives their allotted possession by right of sonship. In other words, because God has made us His children, we have full rights to receive His inheritance. We are His beneficiaries. "And if you

132

are Christ's, then you are Abraham's seed, and heirs according to the promise." (Galatians 3:29)

It is an honor and privilege to serve others under the direction of the Lord. I enjoy working with my clients and seeing them prosper. One day, as I looked at the pile of mail on my desk, I noticed a handwritten letter from my clients, Bill and Holly. With excitement in my heart, I opened their note and read it.

They have come a long way in their journey toward financial freedom. In their note, they expressed their sincere appreciation for everything they had been learning about being good stewards of the resources God blessed them with. They clearly recognized their responsibility of joint ownership with Jesus and were already aligning their ways with the Word of God. They made the quality decision to press onward and not shrink back in fear. I was so pleased to hear about their spiritual and financial progress.

What are you going to do with the resources God has given you?

Summary

1. We are not our own. We belong to God.
2. We earn income, but God enables us.

3. We possess things and have things in our possession, but God owns them.
4. We are joint heirs with Christ and own everything with God.
5. God wants us to partner with Him on this earth to establish His covenant.

And how do we access all this power to get wealth? It comes from believing God, Who lives on the inside of us, and acting on what He says. As we grow in our knowledge of God's Word and trust His way of doing things, we will desire more and more to partner with Him in advancing God's Kingdom here on this earth. Remember, financial freedom begins in your heart, not your bank account.

God wants to trust us with His wealth here on this earth. This is an awesome privilege and opportunity for us to grow and mature in our faith and experience the true financial freedom that pleases God.

Thank you so much for continuing with us on this journey of faith. We appreciate and want to see you prosper in every area of your life. "Beloved, I wish above all things that thou mayest prosper and be in health, even as thy soul prospereth." (3 John 2 KJV)

We are moving on to discover powerful financial revelations that will help us build a godly financial future. We have three more chapters – Giving – Receiving – Managing. Stay with us!

God's Thoughts for Your Journey

Here are some powerful kingdom thoughts to meditate on and let them sink deep into your heart. They have the power to bring victory into your life and finances.

"You shall not remove your neighbor's landmark, which the men of old have set, in your inheritance which you will inherit in the land that the LORD your God is giving you to possess " (Deuteronomy 19:14). Simply put, each individual or family-owned specific plots of land whose boundaries were not to be violated.

"Yours, O LORD, is the greatness, The power and the glory, The victory and the majesty; For all that is in heaven and in earth is Yours; Yours is the kingdom, O LORD, And You are exalted as head over all. Both riches and honor come from You, And You reign over all. In Your hand is power and might; In

Your hand, it is to make great And to give strength to all." (1 Chronicles 29:11-12)

"But he who is joined to the Lord is one spirit with Him." (1 Corinthians 6:17)

Chapter 11

Attitude of Giving

It was a beautiful summer day. The sun was shining brightly, and the temperature was perfect for enjoying the outdoor weather. As I sat in my air-conditioned office looking out the window, I saw the summer scenery inviting me to be a part of it. I thought about going outside for a quick walk when my next appointment arrived early.

My clients, Don and Judy, have been married for over 60 years, and they were the most generous clients I have ever worked with. Every time they came to visit me, they brought a gift. Sometimes, it was sweet chocolates. Other times, it was a fun gift basket, flowers, or tickets to a special local event. This time, they brought me fresh flowers from their garden at home. How nice. They knew how much I enjoyed the sweet-smelling aroma of fresh flowers.

My clients had a generous attitude and it showed

in their relationships with other people. I thank God for the many times I was a recipient of their loving kindness.

I enjoy being on the receiving end of gifts. How about you? You may be familiar with the famous saying, "It is more blessed to give than to receive." Jesus is the originator of the quote, and He is a perfect example of it. "I have shown you in every way, by laboring like this, that you must support the weak. And remember the words of the Lord Jesus, that He said, 'It is more blessed to give than to receive.'" (Acts 20:35)

Jesus is the biggest giver. He gave His only begotten Son. "For God so loved the world that He gave His only begotten Son, that whoever believes in Him should not perish but have everlasting life." (John 3:16). God gave because He loved us. He loved us so much; He gave His Son to die for us. God is love, and love is a giver.

Since we are made in the image of a loving God, we have an attitude of love and generosity in our nature, too. We ought to be generous with our time and treasures. If we tend to struggle with the act of giving, then our hearts may need to change because giving is a biblical concept.

Let's think of some creative ways to be a blessing to others. We could consider wrapping up good quality chocolate bars in decorative paper and writing an encouraging note to accompany them. How about buying some long-stem roses and giving them to folks at the local senior center? We could also consider buying someone's groceries in line at the grocery store or even putting gasoline in some-one's vehicle at the gas station. And if we had the means to do so, we could buy a new car and bless someone else with it. The list could go on and on.

Can you think of any creative ideas or ways you can give gifts and be a blessing to someone else?

Types of Giving

There are many ways we can give to God and others. To simplify the explanation, let's focus on three main categories.

1. The Tithe

The biblical definition of tithe comes from the Hebrew word maaser, which means "tenth part." Tithing in the Bible refers to giving ten percent of one's annual earnings, productions, or possessions. In the Bible, we observe Abraham giving a tithe to Melchizedek, who represents Jesus. Tithing was practiced 430 years before the Mosaic law. "And blessed be God Most High, Who has delivered your enemies into your hand." And he gave him a tithe of all." (Genesis 14:20-21)

Jesus Christ sanctioned tithing. "Woe to you, scribes and Pharisees, hypocrites! For you pay tithe of mint and anise and cummin and have neglected the weightier matters of the law: justice and mercy and faith. These you ought to have done without leaving the others undone." (Matthew 23:23) Jesus gave His official permission or approval of the tithing principle.

Many of us would not consider taking what belongs to someone else. That would be called stealing. Since the tithe belongs to God according to Scripture, then it would be to our benefit to cooperate with His Word. After all, our Lord knows best.

a. "'But the firstborn of the animals, which should be the LORD's firstborn, no man shall dedicate; whether it is an ox or sheep, it is the LORD's." (Leviticus 27:26)

b. "And all the tithe of the land, whether of the seed of the land or of the fruit of the tree, is the LORD's. It is holy to the LORD." (Leviticus 27:30)

Financial freedom begins with giving to God what belongs to Him.

If it wasn't for God, we wouldn't even have the breath in our lungs to breathe. Giving the tithe to

God expresses our love, honor, trust, and appreciation for Him as our Source of life and provision. God says the first and the tithe belong to Him. Then they are His and not ours to spend.

God doesn't need our money or substance in heaven. However, it is a spiritual principle of honoring God while we are living here on this earth. It is a matter of trusting God with our resources.

Financial freedom begins with giving to God what belongs to Him.

There is only one place in the Bible where God challenges us to test or prove His faithfulness, and that is with the tithe. He is serious about this. "Bring all the tithes into the storehouse, that there may be food in My house, and test Me now in this, says the LORD of Hosts, if I will not open for you the windows of heaven and pour out for you a blessing, that there will not be room enough to receive it." (Malachi 3:10).

Giving begins with our tithes to God. When we participate in the tithing principle by faith, we are cooperating with His way of doing things. The tithe is God's idea. He wants to bless us, and when we honor God, it activates a spiritual law in the heavenlies and His abundant blessings are poured out on us.

My personal tithing story is almost too simple to share, but I will tell it anyway. When I learned God wanted me to tithe, I started giving immediately. I didn't argue with Him. Although I didn't fully understand the joyful part of tithing at the time I started, I did understand the willing and obedient part. "If you are willing and obedient, You shall eat the good of the land." (Isaiah 1:19). I gave with a willing heart and was glad I could honor God with my tithe.

Since I began participating in the tithing principle, I have never stopped, and God has always been faithful to supply my needs. And in many cases, He has done exceedingly abundantly above all that I asked or even thought. "Now to Him who is able to do exceedingly abundantly above all that we ask or think, according to the power that works in us." (Ephesians 3:20). After all, God provided the opportunity for me to write this book!

2. Giving to the Poor

Alms is anything given to relieve the poor. It could be money, food, clothing, shelter, etc. God expects us to contribute to the needs of the less fortunate as He leads us by His Holy Spirit.

Giving to the poor is lending to God. "He who has pity on the poor lends to the LORD, and He will repay what he has given." (Proverbs 19:17).

Recently, I heard this story - A few generous men in their church noticed a family that drove a long distance to come to church, and the tires on their vehicle were bald. They knew this family could use some help with their expenses. Those men privately gave money to the church and designated it for this family to purchase tires. The beneficiaries didn't know who provided the funds. That is alms.

A meal bought for a hungry person would be alms. A warm coat bought to protect a child from the cold would be another example. Groceries given anonymously to a family that has no income are alms.

When was the last time you saw a need, was prompted by the Holy Spirit, and quietly filled it?

Have you considered setting aside some money in your budget to be a blessing to others as God brings these special needs to your attention?

3. Making an Investment into the Gospel

Many times, when people think of giving, they immediately think of donating money to the poor to help them in their time of need. And that is Scriptural. As referenced before, when we give to the poor, we are lending to the Lord, and He will repay us what we have given.

However, there is another type of giving that is

important for us to know about. An offering unto the Lord is like investing into His kingdom. It activates the spiritual law of sowing and reaping. "Give, and it will be given to you: good measure, pressed down, shaken together, and running over will be put into your bosom. For with the same measure that you use, it will be measured back to you." (Luke 6:38)

By giving to God and others, we invest treasures in heaven.

Offerings are investing with God, and they will reap a good harvest. They are above and beyond the tithe and are different than alms. Offerings are like giving a free-will gift for specific purposes.

My clients Don and Judy enjoyed the act of giving so much, they made it a lifestyle. No one had to force them to share their wealth. They understood that their act of giving was truly blessing other people and advancing God's Kingdom. Their generous hearts allowed God to bring increase in their finances. The more they increased, the more they were able to give and be a blessing.

By giving to God and others, we invest treasures in heaven. It is a win-win opportunity for everyone – God, the one who gives, and the one who receives. "But store up for yourselves treasures in heaven, where neither moth nor rust destroy and where thieves do not break in nor steal." (Matthew 6:20).

You can't take your money and possessions with you when you die and leave this earth.

All types of giving come from a heart of love and gratitude toward God and compassion for our fellow man.

Money has a Time Limit

Consider 95-year-old Edward, a widower who came into my office one day with a problem...one I'm sure we all may wish we had. He had several homes, expensive cars, and lucrative investments and was still actively enjoying downhill skiing and boating. As a world traveler who loved his scotch and cigars, he was the very image of old worldly success. But when he came into our firm, I saw a prune-faced man with glazed-over eyes. His biggest problem in life was an enormous amount of money that he could only see how to spend on himself. And he was now faced with the decision of how to dispose of all his wealth before he dies.

Edward had spent the one resource he couldn't get more of—time. And now that time was running out, he saw what a poor investment he had made with it. What generous purpose did he have for all the wealth he had accumulated that could have possibly benefited mankind? The answer was "None."

A couple of thoughts immediately came to my

mind: "How many people could he have helped through humanitarian efforts, by sowing into other ministries preaching the gospel of Jesus Christ, or by giving to organizations that are helping the poor?" "I could think of a lot of wonderful people and ministries to bless with it." He hadn't even given God, the Creator of heaven and earth, a thought. His money had no purpose outside of himself.

When I think of Edward now, Luke 12:20-21 (TPT) comes to mind. "God said to him, 'What a fool you are to trust in your riches and not in me. This very night, the messengers of death are demanding to take your life. Then who will get all the wealth you have stored up for yourself?' This is what will happen to all those who fill up their lives with everything but God." What if Edward had a purpose for his wealth besides himself? How might a godly purpose have affected his life and even his influence in the world around him?

I remember attending a funeral one time and overheard someone ask a question about the deceased rich man in the casket. They commented, "I wonder how much money he left?" In my mind, the answer was clear, "All of it!" You can't take any of your money and possessions with you when you die and leave this earth. My husband likes to say humorously, "Have you ever seen a U-Haul following a hearse?" Of course not!

Rewards

Remember, financial freedom begins in your heart, not your bank account. The main reason for giving is because we love God and people and desire to be obedient to His Word. When we partner with God in our giving, we are setting ourselves up for great satisfaction in our hearts and abundant rewards in our finances.

Sometimes, our rewards are noticed directly in our finances through raises, promotions, gifts, etc. At other times, our rewards come through more revelation, knowledge of the Word of God, creative ideas, and new opportunities that increase the love of God in our hearts toward others and multiply our sphere of influence. Prosperity with God has no limits.

Finally, the act of giving increases our love for God because "For where your treasure is, there will your heart be also." (Matthew 6:21). Our heart follows our treasure. If our treasure or resource is spent loving people and spreading the Word of God around the world, then our love for God and those people will increase. Our heart follows our treasure.

Have you been generous with the resources God

has entrusted to you? Consider practicing multiple forms of creative giving this week and experience the joy of generosity in your heart.

Thank you for continuing with us on this powerful financial journey of faith. In the next chapter, we will explore receiving God's promises. Stay with us!

God's Thoughts for Your Journey

Here are some powerful kingdom thoughts to meditate on and let them sink deep into your heart. They have the power to bring victory into your life and finances.

"He who has a generous eye will be blessed, For he gives of his bread to the poor." (Proverbs 22:9)

"For as he thinks in his heart, so is he." (Proverbs 23.7)

"Therefore, I thought it necessary to exhort the brethren to go to you ahead of time and prepare your generous gift beforehand, which you had previously promised, that it may be ready as a matter of generosity and not as a grudging obligation." (2 Corinthians 9:5)

Chapter 12

Receiving God's Promises

It's a snowy winter morning, and the presents are glistening under the Christmas tree. It's as if the neatly wrapped presents are asking to be opened. We almost hear them calling, "Please open me! I'm here! Pick me first!" Ten-year-old Johnny enters the room rubbing his sleepy eyes and beholds the awesome gifts with his name on them, waiting to be grabbed from under the Christmas tree. His big smile is almost fixed on his little face as he receives his first gift in his hands and starts to unwrap it. What joy fills his heart as he opens every one of his precious gifts.

Johnny was so happy and grateful that his wishes were answered and was very pleased with his new presents. Still smiling, he ran happily over to his mom first, who was sitting across the room, and gave her a big hug and kiss on her cheek. His dad was sitting right next to his mom. Johnny looked at his dad and tried to act like a grown-up man by reaching out his hand for a handshake gesture. His father's eyes were so full of love watching his son open his gifts, seeing the joy it brought him, and how thankful he was for everything. He quickly grabbed Johnny's little hand and pulled his son close to his big chest for one of those memorable "bear hugs." Aww! That was a precious moment Johnny remembered for years to come.

As adults and believers in Jesus Christ, we can also be very excited about receiving all the wonderful gifts our heavenly Father has blessed us with as His children. God's eyes are full of love, anticipating our response to His action. The question to ask ourselves is, "Are we positioning ourselves in faith to receive the endless promises God has prepared for us to enjoy in this life?"

How can we give something to someone else if we haven't received it for ourselves first? We can't give away what we don't have in our possession. That's why it's so important to receive from God what belongs to us – both spiritually and physically. We must

Financial freedom includes our ability to receive from God what rightfully belongs to us.

receive the benefits before we can enjoy them and share them with others.

Heirs of God

Financial freedom includes our ability to receive from God what rightfully belongs to us. We are His children, joint heirs with Jesus, and heirs to the promises of God.

> *For as many as are led by the Spirit of God, these are sons of God. For you did not receive the spirit of bondage again to fear, but you received the Spirit of adoption by whom we cry out, "Abba, Father." The Spirit Himself bears witness with our spirit that we are children of God, and if children, then heirs—heirs of God and joint heirs with Christ, if indeed we suffer with Him, that we may also be glorified together. (Romans 8:14-17)*

Remember how Johnny freely received the presents from his parents at Christmas time? We, too, can freely receive from our heavenly Father because we are His children. And we don't have to wait until Christmas to do this. We can experience the joy of receiving God's promises today.

The term "heirs of God" emphasizes our relationship to God the Father—we are His children. Johnny didn't earn his gifts by performing great chores.

They were given to him because of his relationship with his parents. Gifts are not earned; they are freely given. With his childlike faith, Johnny grabbed the presents under the Christmas tree with his name on them. He tore off the wrapping paper, opened the boxes, and enjoyed every minute of it.

In the same way, God has many blessings with our name on them, waiting for us to grab them by faith in His Word and enjoy them. God is a loving Father; He wants the best for us and is delighted when we prosper in every area of our life. "Let them shout for joy and be glad, Who favor my righteous cause; And let them say continually, "Let the LORD be magnified, Who has pleasure in the prosperity of His servant." (Psalm 35:27).

Right of Sonship

Ten-year-old Johnny may have looked at all his Christmas gifts under the tree that morning and thought in his little mind that he had received everything he wanted. But there is so much more available to him now and in the years to come through his relationship with Jesus.

Think of Who we are heirs with—Jesus Christ, God's only begotten Son. Begotten is an archaic term referring to when a child is the only offspring of his or her father. Jesus is the only offspring of God the Father. Thus, Jesus is the only natural "heir" to God's throne.

Jesus' inheritance is everything that is God's, which is everything in existence.

We are also God's heirs and joint heirs with Jesus Christ. Just as Jesus is the heir to God's throne, we are also heirs to God's throne. Just as Jesus' inheritance is everything that is God's, our inheritance is also everything that is God's. And what belongs to God? Everything...in the entire universe. It's all God's property. ALL of it.

It will take eternity for us to receive everything God has for us. The good news is that we can start learning how to receive from God once we accept Jesus as our Lord and Savior and become born again. "That if you confess with your mouth the Lord Jesus and believe in your heart that God has raised Him from the dead, you will be saved. For with the heart, one believes unto righteousness, and with the mouth, confession is made unto salvation." (Romans 10:9-10).

Get Ready to Receive

Confessing Jesus as our Lord and Savior and believing in our hearts is just the beginning. Every blessing from God is received the same way—confess with our mouth and believe with our heart.

Faith requires action. We can't just sit at home in our "reclining chair", confess the Word, and expect it to produce results without any corresponding action. It would be like a farmer wanting a harvest and just buying the seeds and confessing over them but never taking any action to plant them in the ground. "Just as the body is dead without breath, so also faith is dead without good works." (James 2:26 NLT)

How do we put ourselves in a position to receive from God? God has already done His part by purchasing our blessings for us. Although we are entitled to our inheritance, it is not automatic. Here are some areas that can help put us in a position to receive from God.

The Faithful Act of Giving

The faithful act of giving opens opportunities for God to shower us with blessings and provisions. "But seek first the kingdom of God and his righteousness, and all these things shall be given to you." (Matthew 6:33). No, we are not purchasing any of God's blessings by our giving. As we make the quality decision to put God first place in our hearts and lives, He can get things to us by faith. Once we receive the blessings He has already provided for us, then we can freely enjoy them and share them with others as the Lord directs.

It pleases God when we give out of a joyful heart of love for others. God loves a cheerful giver, not one who gives grudgingly or out of necessity. "So let each one give as he purposes in his heart, not grudgingly or of necessity; for God loves a cheerful giver." (2 Corinthians 9:7).

Our desire in this journey is to be in a position of financial freedom to partner with God, finance His Kingdom purposes, and establish His covenant on this earth. "And you shall remember the LORD your God, for it is He who gives you power to get wealth, that He may establish His covenant which He swore to your fathers, as it is this day." (Deuteronomy 8:18)

Spiritual Living

We can receive from God through our spiritual living. When we take responsibility and align ourselves with God's way of doing things, we put ourselves "under the spout where the blessings pour out." Our obedience to God is not to coerce Him to move on our behalf and bless us. God has already moved on our behalf and given us all things that pertain unto life and godliness. We simply cooperate with Him by faith and action in what Jesus has already done.

As His divine power has given to us all things that pertain to life and godliness, through the knowledge of Him who called us by glory and virtue, by which have been given to us exceedingly great and precious promises, that through these you may be partakers of the divine nature, having escaped the corruption that is in the world through lust. (2 Peter 1:3-4)

Ten-year-old Johnny did not have to do everything right and live perfectly to receive his presents. His gifts were already provided for by his parents. What Johnny did was cooperate with his parents' authority and do things their way. As a result, the young boy was in the right place at the right time and was able to receive all that his parents had in store for him on Christmas morning.

Diligent Labor

We can receive God's provisions for us through our diligent labor. This does not mean that we are working for the promises of God. It means we are putting action to what we believe. God can bless what we put our hands to.

"The LORD will open to you His good treasure, the heavens, to give the rain to your land in its season and to bless all the work of your hand. You shall lend to many nations, but you shall not borrow." (Deuteronomy 28:12)

"And let the beauty of the LORD our God be upon us, And establish the work of our hands for us; Yes, establish the work of our hands." (Psalm 90:17)

It feels good to work diligently and accomplish something worthwhile. "For when we were with you, we commanded you that if any will not work, neither shall he eat. For we hear that there are some among you who live in idleness, mere busybodies, not working at all. Now, concerning those who are such, we command and exhort by our Lord Jesus Christ that they quietly work and eat their own bread." (2 Thessalonians 3:10-12).

Johnny did not have to work for his presents. However, the young boy chose to have his own newspaper route in his neighborhood and was able to save enough money to buy his parents some nice Christmas gifts. Johnny exercised the principle of diligent labor; God blessed the fruit of his hands, he received income from his job, and he was able to purchase gifts to give to others.

Sowing and Reaping

We can receive or reap a good harvest if we plant or sow good seeds. It is one of God's spiritual laws.

"Be not deceived. God is not mocked. For whatever a man sows, that shall he also reap." (Galatians 6:7).

The kinds of seeds we plant will determine the type of harvest we will produce. If a farmer plants tomato seeds, he will reap tomato plants that will produce vine-ripe tomatoes. What kinds of seeds are we planting in our hearts and lives – anger, bitterness, and strife, or love, peace, and joy? (Please refer to chapters 2-9 on how to be free from the financial bondages holding our hearts hostage.)

We can receive or reap a good harvest if we plant or sow good seeds.

Little Johnny's heart was filled with joy and laughter. He appreciated everything his parents provided for him. He also had a great sense of humor and would often make his parents laugh. He sowed good seeds of joy and reaped many happy days on this earth.

We don't have to wait until we have millions of dollars to begin giving. We can start with what we have, even if it is one dollar. God needs something to multiply. He cannot increase nothing. If we want a good harvest, we must plant good seeds in faith from our heart of love.

If you would like to sow into advancing the Kingdom of God, ask the Lord for seed to sow, and He will provide it. God gives seed to the one who is willing to sow. "Now may He who supplies seed to the sower, and bread for food, supply and multiply the seed you have sown and increase the fruits of your righteousness." (2 Corinthians 9:10).

Are you ready to position yourself to receive from God? Remember, financial freedom begins in your heart, not your bank account.

Thank you for continuing with us on this amazing journey of faith. We are building inner strength through the Word of God and are ready to tackle our final chapter, Managing Your Finances. Stay steadfast. You can do it!

God's Thoughts for Your Journey

Here are some powerful kingdom thoughts to meditate on and let them sink deep into your heart. They have the power to bring victory into your life and finances.

"Ask, and it will be given to you; seek, and you will find; knock, and it will be opened to you. For everyone who asks receives, and he who seeks finds, and to him who knocks it will be opened." (Matthew 7:7-8)

"I tell you, you can pray for anything, and if you believe that you've received it, it will be yours." (Mark 11:24 NLT)

"Faith is the assurance of things you have hoped for, the absolute conviction that there are realities you've never seen. It was by faith that our forebears were approved. Through faith we understand that the universe was created by the word of God; everything we now see was fashioned from that which is invisible." (Hebrews 11:1-3 VOICE)

Chapter 13

Managing Your Finances

The wind is howling through the snow-covered trees on this chilly day in New England. We received 18 inches of snowfall during the night. On this brisk morning, the skiers, who are on vacation, are happy because they can now venture out and explore the new snow-covered slopes. To them, the snow means an opportunity to have fun and get some exercise. Other people who are required to shovel their driveways and clear their cars and driveways to get to work are not as excited about this new weather-related chore as the skiers are.

The same is true when it comes to managing our money. Some people like it, and others do not. My clients Bill and Holly were not initially excited about managing their finances when their first consultation revealed a significant loss. However, after they realized it was essential to their spiritual growth and success in life, as well as in their finances, they were willing to face the facts and learn how to be good stewards with their God-given resources.

What comes to your mind when you think of managing your money? Maybe budgeting or struggling to make ends meet? Or do you think of hiring a financial professional to invest your money for you?

I've heard some successful financial experts say that one of the biggest lessons they've learned when it comes to managing their money is to "spend less than they earn and do it over a long period of time." It sounds so simple, yet it can be challenging at times. Life happens, and our unproductive habits and uncontrolled emotions can also get in the way of our best plans.

Stewardship

The better we become at skillful money management and stewardship, the more we will see how it influences our prosperity in a huge way.

Enjoying financial freedom involves our willingness to take good care of the resources God has given us. It's a simple, heartwarming respect toward the things God has put in our lives, whether it is our jobs, money, or relationships. Management starts with a watchful, caring heart that's willing to learn the practical and spiritual ways to please God with what He's given us.

When 10-year-old Johnny was given a new bicycle by his parents, he showed his sincere appreciation for it, enjoyed it, washed it, maintained it, locked it while it was in public places, and always stored it in a place sheltered from the harsh weather. Can you imagine the joy he brought to his parents when they saw how he took good care of the things they gave him?

Enjoying financial freedom involves our willingness to take good care of the resources God has given us.

Now consider this—what if Johnny took the gift of his new bicycle for granted and complained about the features? What if he didn't care about all the sacrifices his parents made to save their money and buy it for him? What if he didn't make any effort to maintain it and didn't lock it safely in public places? Let's say he constantly left it outside for the rain and snowstorms to weather it.

It brings sorrow to parents when they see their children place no value on the gifts they have worked so hard to provide for them. On the other hand, it pleases parents to see their children manage their blessings wisely. The same is true with our heavenly Father.

Why would God want to bless us with more resources when we don't even appreciate the ones He has given us right now? If we are overspending our money recklessly today, not saving anything, or not giving into God's kingdom with a willing and purposeful heart, then what would happen if God gave us more? Our present money management habits are an indication of how we will handle more money in the future. Of course, if we repent, renew our minds, and become good stewards, then our poor habits can be changed into prosperous ones.

If we are not faithful with the little He has entrusted to us, what makes us think God wants to trust us with even more? "He who has a slack hand becomes poor, But the hand of the diligent makes rich." (Proverbs 10:4). Managing our finances wisely is a big deal to God, and I believe it needs to be a priority with us, too.

Faithfulness

Another way of looking at managing our finances is being faithful with what God has entrusted to us now. I have fond memories of my precious clients, James, and Kyleigh, who exhibited sincere attitudes of gratitude, and were so determined to be good

166

stewards with their money. They saw the value in being faithful with God's resources and carried that attitude into every area of their lives.

At the grocery store, James and Kyleigh considered even the little choices and purchases they made before proceeding to the cash register. They did not fall prey to impulse buying. When they treated a friend to lunch, they did it with love and excellence. And giving in the offering plate at church was accompanied by their cheerful heart. They desired to be faithful, listen, and obey the voice and wisdom of God, and act accordingly. As a result, they grew in greater riches and more important responsibilities during the years I knew them.

"The one who faithfully manages the little he has been given will be promoted and trusted with greater responsibilities. But those who cheat with the little they have been given will not be considered trustworthy to receive more. If you have not handled the riches of this world with integrity, why should you be trusted with the eternal treasures of the spiritual world?" (Luke 16:10-11 TPT).

Blessings flow to us and through us from our willingness and obedience to follow God's instructions. "If you are willing and obedient, you shall eat the good of the land; But if you refuse and rebel, you shall be devoured with the sword; for the mouth of the Lord has spoken it." (Isaiah 1:19-20).

I am not referring to God's promises being dependent upon our self-efforts or obedience to perform all the laws perfectly. The Law helped us realize it was not humanly possible to keep all the commandments and that we needed a Savior.

Under the New Covenant, Jesus fulfilled the Law, and all the promises are yes and amen to us. Our obedience is now one of faith in what Jesus has already done for us. When we put action to our faith, we are being willing and obedient.

Abraham is a perfect example of one who was strong in his faith. Romans 4:20-21 says, "He staggered not at the promise of God through unbelief; but was strong in faith, giving glory to God; and being fully persuaded that, what he has promised, he was able also to perform." The Bible tells us that Abraham believed God's promise and that the promise was fulfilled through Jesus Christ.

If we believe God the way that Abraham believed God, we too can inherit the same promise and blessing of the Spirit through faith. "And if you are Christ's, then you are Abraham's seed, and heirs according to the promise." (Galatians 3:29).

What is The Blessing God promised Abraham?

'I will make you into a great nation,
and I will bless you;
I will make your name great,
and you will be a blessing.

I will bless those who bless you,
and whoever curses you I will curse;
and all peoples on earth
will be blessed through you.' (Genesis 12:1-3)

The promises of God are available to us, who are Abraham's seed, through faith and not by the works of the Law. Please note that the blessings of God are not automatic. They will not just fall on us like ripe cherries falling off a tree. We still have a responsibility to receive the promises of God by faith and act on them. Our part is to believe what God's Word says and then respond with corresponding action.

Here are a couple of practical examples of how we can manage our affairs in God's way.

Pay Bills Promptly

Paying our bills promptly is scriptural. "Do not say to your neighbor, "Go, and come again, and tomorrow I will give it;" when you have it with you." (Proverbs 3:28).

If someone attempts to collect payments from us, and we have it in our possession but refuse to pay them and instead tell them to come back tomorrow, we need to seriously ask ourselves, "What are we waiting for?" Let's put ourselves in the vendor or bill collector's shoes. If the same amount is owed to us, wouldn't we want to receive the money owed to us on time? I know I would.

Save and Invest Wisely

Another way of managing our resources is through saving and investing wisely. "There is treasure to be desired and oil in the dwelling of the wise; but a foolish man squanders it." (Proverbs 21:20).

Success starts with hearing the voice of God clearly in our hearts and then following His specific instructions. Being led by the Holy Spirit is being led by godly wisdom, and that will result in godly success.

Many of us can easily fall prey to our fickle emotions, insecurities, fears, or lusts to get rich quickly and act on those unstable sources. Financial bondages are the hidden issues of our hearts that can stop us from increasing God's way. Overcoming these bondages, as mentioned in the previous chapters, is vital to our journey toward financial freedom.

Let's remember to put God first in our lives and in our finances.

I highly recommend having a savings account. It is scriptural to have a storehouse. "Honor the Lord with your capital and sufficiency [from righteous labors] and with the first fruits of all your income. So shall your storage places be filled with plenty, and your vats shall be overflowing with new wine." (Proverbs 3:9-10 AMPC).

And remember, as some successful financial experts say, that one of the biggest lessons they've learned when it comes to managing their money is to "spend less than they earn and do it over a long period of time." That can result in having a storehouse. Reducing expenses as appropriate and deciding on the amount of money we can reasonably afford to save every month is wise management of our resources and a good stewardship practice.

After our basic needs are met and a savings account is in place, then longer-term investments can be considered.

Let's remember to put God first in our lives and in our finances. According to the Word of God, He wants us to invest into His kingdom first, then everything else will follow. "But seek first the kingdom of God and His righteousness, and all these things shall be added to you." (Matthew 6:33).

Get Out of Debt

It is God's will for you to be out of debt. "Render to all men their dues. [Pay] taxes to whom taxes are due, revenue to whom revenue is due, respect to whom respect is due, and honor to whom honor is due. Keep out of debt and owe no man anything, except to love one another; for he who loves his neighbor [who practices loving others] has fulfilled the Law [relating to one's fellowmen, meeting all its requirements]." (Romans 13:7-8 AMPC)

In this Scripture, Paul is talking about finances and love. When we are out of debt financially, the only thing left is for us to love one another, and thereby fulfill the commandment of God.

"When you run in debt, you give to another power over your liberty." (Franklin)

1. Here are some simple steps to get out of debt:
2. Set a goal to be debt-free. Write the vision.
3. Make a list of all the debts you owe. Then, pick one debt at a time, set it as a target, and pay it off.
4. Add no new debts.
5. Be single-minded. Purpose in your heart to get out of debt.

There are many reasons to keep out of debt. (My website has some teachings on the Reasons to Keep Out of Debt.) The best reason I can think of is that we will be free to partner with God, impact the lives of other people, and give more resources into the

Kingdom of God for the purpose of preaching of the Gospel. We will no longer be encumbered with debt and can make a significant impact into the lives of many people for eternity's sake.

Summary

Bill and Holly became very successful in their journey toward financial freedom since the first wintery day they arrived in my office facing a deficit of $10,000. During the time I knew them, they navigated through turbulent financial and emotional waters and landed safely on the banks of unity and peace in their marriage. They overcame many financial bondages, changed their hearts to follow God's way of handling their finances, and emerged winners in their lives. They recognized that their true source of financial freedom started with the Word of God firmly planted in their hearts.

God is preparing His people, like Bill and Holly, to fund the end-time harvest of souls by establishing His covenant on this earth. "And you shall remember the LORD your God, for it is He who gives you power to get wealth, that He may establish His covenant which He swore to your fathers, as it is this day." (Deuteronomy 8:18) And you can be a part of establishing God's covenant too.

My desire is to see you move into God's will for

your finances and experience the freedom to participate in this great event. Remember, financial freedom begins in your heart, not your bank account.

My prayer for you is, "Beloved, I pray that you
may prosper in all things and be in health, just as
your soul prospers." (3 John 2)

Thank you for your steadfastness in continuing
with us on this life changing journey of Financial
Freedom Through the Word of God. There are more
revelations still to come from the Author and Fin-
isher of our faith.

I pray this book has brought a fresh awareness to
your heart in your path toward financial freedom.
When our hearts are free, then we are no longer in
bondage. We are free to give. We are free to receive.
We are free to manage all the goodness that we
are receiving. And finally, we are free to love God,
partner with Him, and help others by going beyond

ourselves and expanding God's Kingdom on this earth. Will you join us?

God's Thoughts for Your Journey

Here are some powerful kingdom thoughts to meditate on and let them sink deep into your heart. They have the power to bring victory into your life and finances.

―――

"To those who use well what they are given, even more, will be given, and they will have an abundance. But from those who do nothing, even what little they have will be taken away." (Matthew 25:29 NLT)

"[Remember] this: he who sows sparingly and grudgingly will also reap sparingly and grudgingly, and he who sows generously that blessings may come to someone] will also reap generously and with blessings. Let each one [give] as he has made up his own mind and purposed in his heart, not reluctantly or sorrowfully or under compulsion, for God loves (He takes pleasure in, prizes above other things, and is unwilling to abandon or to do without) a cheerful (joyous, "prompt to do it") giver [whose heart is in his giving]." (2 Corinthians 9:6-7 AMPC)

"Don't be selfish; don't try to impress others. Be humble, thinking of others as better than yourselves. Don't look out only for your own interests, but take an interest in others, too." (Philippians 2:3-4 NLT)

Prayer for Salvation and Baptism in the Holy Spirit

Heavenly Father, I come to You in the Name of Jesus. Your word says, "Whoever calls on the name of the LORD shall be saved." (Acts 2:21). I am calling on You. I pray and ask Jesus to come into my heart and be Lord over my life, according to Romans 10:9-10. "That if you confess with your mouth the Lord Jesus and believe in your heart that God has raised Him from the dead, you will be saved. For with the heart, one believes unto righteousness, and with the mouth, confession is made unto salvation." I do that now. I confess that Jesus is Lord, and I believe in my heart that God raised Him from the dead.

I am now reborn! I am a Christian—a child of Almighty God! I am saved! You also said in Your Word, "If you then, being evil, know how to give good gifts to your children, how much more will your heavenly Father give the Holy Spirit to those who ask Him!" (Luke 11:13). I am also asking You to fill me with the Holy Spirit. Holy Spirit, rise from within me as I praise God. I fully expect to speak with other tongues as You give me the utterance. (Acts 2:4) In Jesus' Name. Amen!

Begin to praise God for filling you with the Holy Spirit. Speak those words and syllables you receive— not in your own language, but the language given to you by the Holy Spirit. You must use your own voice. God will not force you to speak. Don't be concerned with how it sounds. It is a heavenly language! Continue with the blessing God has given you and pray in the spirit every day.

You are a born-again, Spirit-filled believer. You'll never be the same!

I encourage you to find a good church that boldly preaches God's Word and obeys it. Becoming part of a church family who will love and care for you, as you love and care for them, is vital to your spiritual growth.

We need to be connected to each other. This synergy increases our strength together with God, resulting in victory. It is our heavenly Father's plan for us to be in unity with Him on this earth and in eternity.

Please share your relationship with Jesus, and this book too, with others so more people can be set free!

About the Author

Diane Grubis is passionate about teaching the Word of God and hosting the Epic Conversations program, which is a product of Diane Grubis Ministries.

Her Epic Conversations program is building God's Kingdom by taking ordinary people's lives and magnifying Jesus in and through them. The heartwarming stories of her guests make us laugh, make us cry, and always help us to grow in God in ways you couldn't have imagined!

Diane's teaching ministry was birthed out of a word from God that Diane received during an early morning prayer meeting in 1990. The spirit of the Lord said, "Sow the tithing principle into the heart of God's people." She began with a course entitled, Financial Freedom Through the Word of God." In 2019, she and her husband expanded their outreach of teaching the Word of God to an online audience via a YouTube channel with guests called Epic Conversations.

She is a decisive professional who communicates effectively, has the gift of hospitality, and has been blessed with the ability to teach and exhort others.

Diane attended Life Christian University and received her Doctor of Philosophy in theology; she attended Charis Bible College and received her master's in biblical studies. She is a licensed minister; she attended Anna Maria College and received her MBA—master's in business administration.

In 2021, she started her own ministry, Diane Grubis Ministries, as a tax-exempt 501(c)(3) corporation. She grew up in Massachusetts and now lives in Colorado with her husband, John.

Website: https://dianegrubis.com

Email: diane@dianegrubis.com

YouTube Channel: https://www.youtube.com/channel/UCx7-uWALHILpADrn_9dzXzQ

Diane Grubis Ministries | 3246 Centennial Blvd #328 | Colorado Springs, CO 80907

Diane Grubis

M I N I S T R I E S

EPIC CONVERSATIONS